BANANAS

Also by Peter Chapman

The Goalkeeper's History of Britain

BANANAS

HOW THE UNITED FRUIT COMPANY SHAPED THE WORLD

★

Edinburgh · New York · Melbourne

First published in Great Britain in 2007 by
Canongate Books Ltd., Edinburgh, Scotland

Printed in the United States of America

ISBN 978-1-84767-194-3
eISBN 978-0-8021-9200-4

Grove Atlantic
154 West 14th Street
New York, NY 10011

Distributed by Publishers Group West

groveatlantic.com

16 17 18 19 9 8 7 6

To Marie, Alex and Pepe

Acknowledgements

Special thanks to: Sally (Holloway), for applying shape and getting it to the outside world, and to Felicity, Michele and all in the Felicity Bryan office; to Andy (Miller) for his acute editing skills and enthusiasm for the subject, to Jamie for (on a whim and late on a Friday night) going with the idea, to Dan, Helen and everyone at Canongate for their help; to Clive (Priddle) for first spotting the story and to Tim (Whitfield) for his friendship and support; to Marie I for her concern, Marie II for her involvement and patience ('is it finished yet?'), Bill, Sue (and the boys) for helping whenever possible and my sister Maria and my mother for their support over many years. A much belated note of thanks goes to the University of Sussex, not least to John Maclean, Robin Murray and Roderick Ogley, and to Nick Barr, Ray Barrell, Richard Jackman, Steve Nickell and my other economics teachers in the late 1970s at the London School of Economics. That said, I have intended this book as a popular account, rather than scholarly analysis of United Fruit and kept footnotes to the bearest minimum. A select bibliography is at the back.

Contents

List of Characters

Selected characters in order of appearance:

Eli Black: Last chief of United Fruit, his suicide in 1975 prompted a furious reaction against the company.

United Fruit Company: Multi-national colossus, famously known as the 'Octopus'. Mysteriously disappeared following Eli Black's death.

Fidel Castro: Cuban guerrilla, upbringing paid for by United Fruit, which leased land to his father to grow sugar. Seized power in 1959 viewing the company as a 'grave social problem'.

Gabriel García Márquez: Nobel Prize-winning author, born in the company's Colombian banana zone near the time of the 1928 Santa Marta massacre.

Anastasio Somoza: Dictator of Nicaragua, deposed in 1979, whose family had enjoyed for many years a close confluence of interests with the company.

Carmen Miranda: Brazilian entertainer. Enjoyed huge popularity in the US during the 'Good Neighbor' years of the 1930s and 40s and inspired many in her 'tutti-frutti' hat.

Dr José María Castro: Nineteenth-century president of Costa Rica whose wife, Pacífica, designed the national flag and whose daughter, Cristina, married United Fruit boss Minor Keith.

General Tomás Guardia: Brought the railroad to Costa Rica in the 1870s and inadvertently opened the way to United Fruit.

Minor Keith: Keeper of the company store in Costa Rica who went on to lead the company in the early twentieth century as the 'uncrowned king of Central America'.

Andrew Preston: Joined with Minor Keith in 1899 and ran United Fruit from its headquarters in Boston, Massachusetts.

Manuel Estrada Cabrera: Dictator of Guatemala who seized power in 1898 and ceded much of it to United Fruit six years later.

Samuel Zemurray: The Banana Man. Organised the Honduran invasion of 1911 and was central to company affairs for over forty years.

Theodore Roosevelt: US president who shared United Fruit's expansionist views in the early twentieth century. Argued with the company during the building of the Panama Canal.

O. Henry: Author, coined the term 'banana republic' in 1904 and portrayed US presence in Central America as a life of loveable rogues.

General Manuel Bonilla: Honduran dictator, deposed in 1907. Restored to presidency by Zemurray afer 1911 invasion.

Lee Christmas: Led the 1911 invasion of Honduras alongside his colleague Guy 'Machine-gun' Molony.

Woodrow Wilson: US president, 1913–21, who crossed swords with United Fruit and its well-bred Boston allies.

John Foster Dulles: Took a close interest in United Fruit affairs in Central America from the First World War and became its legal adviser. Went on to be US secretary of state in the 1950s when his brother Allen Dulles led the Central Intelligence Agency (CIA); both instrumental in the 1954 overthrow of Guatemala's elected government, which had made enemies of United Fruit.

General Jorge Ubico: Guatemalan Bonapartist dictator who in the 1930s allowed United Fruit to spread across the Central American isthmus to the Pacific.

Franklin D. Roosevelt: US president, 1933–45, who wanted to boost trade between the US and Latin America to help alleviate the economic Depression of the 1930s. Furious with United Fruit for its preference for doing business with Nazi Germany.

General Smedley Butler: Marine, unmasked a big-business plot against President Franklin D. Roosevelt in the 1930s. Blamed himself for the 'rape' of the Central American republics.

Edward Bernays: Self-professed propaganda guru, the 'Father of Public Relations'. Orchestrated 1950s US public opinion for the overthrow of Guatemala's elected government.

Senator Joseph McCarthy: US investigator of the 1950s 'red menace'. Shared the company's world view.

President Jacobo Arbenz: Guatemalan leader, adversary of the company and deposed in the 1954 coup. Alleged to be dominated by his radical wife, María.

E. Howard Hunt: Ubiquitous CIA man whose career closely paralleled that of United Fruit in the 1950s and 60s. Jailed in the 1970s for his role in the Watergate scandal.

José 'Pepe' Figueres: Costa Rican democratic leader who invited United Fruit to pay for his country's welfare state, and got away with it.

Jack Peurifoy: Brash US ambassador who supervised the 1954 coup from the Guatemalan end.

Richard Nixon: US vice-president in the 1950s. Went on to be president and resigned in 1974 as a result of 'Watergate'.

Ernesto 'Che' Guevara: Tried to rally armed resistance to the company in Guatemala before making off to join Fidel Castro's guerrillas preparing their effort to take power in Cuba.

John F. Kennedy: US president who assumed office in 1961 and failed, shortly after, to give full backing to United Fruit and others at the Bay of Pigs invasion of Cuba. Assassinated in 1963.

Jimmy Carter: US president, 1977–81, who advocated improved human rights in Central America. Regarded at home as a 'weak' leader.

General Omar Torrijos: Panamanian leader and opponent of United Fruit. Negotiated to have the US cede control of the Panama Canal. Died in a plane crash in 1981.

Ronald Reagan: US president in the 1980s who fought the Cold War's last battle on United Fruit's old Central American territory.

John Negroponte: US ambassador in 1980s Honduras who said he was not turning the country into 'an armed camp'. Led a successful diplomatic career and came out of retirement for the 2003 Iraq invasion and aftermath.

1
From the Memory of Men

A policeman called to the spot spoke of the selfishness of 'jumpers'. Locked in their own minds, they didn't think of anyone 'down below'. This one killed himself in the Manhattan rush hour and could have taken any number of people with him. Glass fell amid the traffic, the body itself landing near a ramp used by vehicles of an office of the US postal service. Postmen came out to help emergency workers clear up.

At dawn on Monday, February 3, 1975 a man had thrown himself from the forty-fourth floor of the Pan-American building on New York's Park Avenue. The 'jumper' was soon identified as Eli Black, aged fifty-three and head of United Brands, a large food corporation. A little over five years earlier, after one of the largest ever share deals on the US stock market, Black had taken over the United Fruit Company. He had absorbed one of the most famous – if not infamous – companies in the world into the United Brands group.

United Fruit's business was bananas. From bananas it had built an empire. The small states of Central America to the south of the US had come to be known as the 'banana republics': Guatemala, El Salvador, Honduras, Nicaragua, Costa Rica and Panama. United Fruit's reach extended to Belize – former British Honduras – and to Caribbean islands such as Jamaica and Cuba. In South America, Colombia and Ecuador had come under its sway. A company more powerful than many nation states, it was a law unto itself and accustomed to regarding the republics as its private fiefdom.

Why then had Black killed himself? Business was not thriving. A new banana disease had struck United Fruit's plantations in the early 1970s. The Middle East war of October 1973 had taken its toll on company fortunes: OPEC, the cartel of oil-producing countries, had multiplied the price of oil several times, which had hit the world as a whole but had had a particular effect on United Fruit. Latin America's banana-producing countries had set up a cartel of their own: UPEB, the union of banana-exporting countries. UPEB had promptly declared 'banana war' on United Fruit to get more money out of the company. From the money it made, United Fruit had always paid the producers the bare minimum. In 1974 nature had taken a hand. Hurricane Fifi had devastated the company's plantations in Honduras. Hurricanes were an occupational hazard in banana farming but Fifi was of unprecedented force – a wind of near biblical proportion. All these factors had contributed to United Fruit's current malaise.

Strangely, the business world suggested another dimension to Black's suicide. Amid the expressions of sympathy at his funeral, in the press and around New York's financial centre of Wall Street, some wondered whether Black's ethics had killed him. He was a man of exceptional morality, it was said. A devout Jew, he was from ten generations of rabbis. Thirty years before, Black had been ordained and had served a community in Long Island. He had subsequently ventured into business – he was a brilliant salesman and had made some spectacular deals – but had retained his principles.

At Christmas 1972 an earthquake in Nicaragua had destroyed

the centre of Managua, the capital city. Under Black's direction, United Fruit was quick to send aid. A popular US cause of the time was the fate of Latin American farm workers, who worked in the US in poor conditions and for very low pay. Black opened negotiations with their unions. Many of his business associates considered him mad for such apparent generosity of spirit. Soon after his death, an article in the *Wall Street Journal* suggested it might mean there was no place for a person of high moral standards in an uncompromising financial world.

In 1975 I was a student at the University of Sussex. I am sorry to say that Black's death struck me as bizarrely comic. The idea of anyone who ran United Fruit occupying the moral high ground seemed absurd. The company's long history rendered it the ultimate 'corporate nasty'. It changed governments when it didn't like them, like the one in Guatemala in 1954 that had wanted to donate some of United Fruit's unused land to landless peasants. In 1961 United Fruit ships sailed to the Bay of Pigs in Cuba in an effort to overthrow Fidel Castro. As far back as 1928 the company was implicated in the massacre of hundreds of striking workers in Colombia. Gabriel García Márquez had written about the strike in *One Hundred Years of Solitude*. Born just before the massacre, he had taken the name of his fictional banana zone of 'Macondo' from that of a United Fruit plantation near his home in Aracataca.

In the 1970s, information from Latin America was still surprisingly scant. At the time, I saw television news footage of the earthquake in Nicaragua; I don't think I'd ever heard the country's name said before. A man was climbing across the ruins; he was overweight and doing so with difficulty, but he was consoling the bereaved and dispossessed. He was Anastasio Somoza, the president. There had been other Somozas before him and another Anastasio, his son, was waiting to succeed him. The president ran many of Nicaragua's businesses and it was amazing he had any time to run the country at all. It had already been speculated that he would do well from the anticipated flood of earthquake relief funds.

Soon after, I caught another programme, a rare BBC documentary on Central America, specifically Honduras. For the first time that I can recall, the United Fruit Company was mentioned. The company, it was reported, had built several hundred miles of railway on its plantations in the distant north-east of the country on the Atlantic coast. The Honduran capital, Tegucigalpa, by contrast was on the high central plateau. For many years the city had been promised a railway of its own, and it had duly given the United Fruit Company a lot of land on which to grow its bananas, but the line had never materialised. Tegucigalpa, therefore, was one of the few capitals of the world, possibly the only one, that didn't have its own railway station.

As for bananas, I already had some interest because I had spent two months on a banana kibbutz in Israel, on the border with Syria, at the southern reaches of the Israeli-occupied Golan Heights, and Jordan. Its plantation was a few minutes' drive by tractor from the kibbutz's residential buildings, and formed a kind of detached enclave on the outer edges of kibbutz life. It was far nearer the neighbouring Jordanian village and only a few yards from the frontier wire. The banana plants grew to about five metres high, their fronds arching over us to make for a lot of pleasantly refracted sunlight. Mostly, however, the plantation was a sweaty and contained world. Tarantulas and scorpions allegedly lurked in each stem of bananas, though they failed to reveal themselves let alone bite or sting. We were warned against snacking on fallen fruit, especially any with split skin, in case it had received the attention of rats, which, it was said, liberally pissed around in the plantation by night.

The work involved humping banana stems of some forty kilos each from banana plant to tractor trailer for six hours a day. Just easy enough not to be onerous, it was my first experience of the 'dignity of labour'. The pay amounted to only a few pence a day but I quite enjoyed being out of the world of money. Not all those with me agreed: 'fucking communists', said Irwin, my co-worker from Brooklyn.

Such experience of the world I took with me to university. With fees paid and a government grant, I went to Sussex, a detached enclave in its own right, its campus carved out of the forest on the English south coast and devoted to theoretical improvement. I did a course in International Relations. When it eventually came to writing my final thesis I chose the case of United Fruit and the banana republics.

'Banana republic' was a familiar enough term. It had seemed inoffensively jokey, at worst a form of shorthand for political and economic mismanagement, probably with corruption thrown in, plus an element of national dependence on some large external force. It turned out, however, to be a more patronising and derogatory term than I had imagined, at least as viewed by the countries and people to whom it was applied. It was used as if it described their original state, while saying very little of what role any aforementioned large external force may have played in creating or exacerbating their predicament.

By its actions, United Fruit had invented the concept and reality of the banana republic.*

One thing I learned during my research was that such a republic didn't have to produce bananas to qualify for the title. Nicaragua, for example, did not grow bananas in any great commercial quantity. The country's banana republicanism resided in the happy coincidence of views enjoyed by the ruling Somoza family, United Fruit and the US. The Somozas had been first to offer their services to assist in both the Guatemalan coup in 1954 and the Bay of Pigs invasion in 1961. Washington regarded the Somozas' army (well-equipped with US arms) and United Fruit as forces for stability that kept Central America subdued.

By the mid-1970s, when I was writing my thesis, multinational corporations had become a theme of the age. Salvador Allende's left-wing government had been overthrown in Chile by the armed forces led by General Augusto Pinochet. The International Telephone & Telegraph Corporation (ITT), a US company that had big interests in Chile, was thought to be behind it. At the same time, OPEC's oil price rises had caused crisis around the world, yet the oil companies had emerged with huge profits. Barclays Bank, meanwhile, based in Britain, was making big money out of apartheid in South Africa.

But in all such corporate practices United Fruit had been there before. In order to price-fix, United Fruit hadn't troubled with setting up cartels, it just did the job on its own

* Never let such sober interpretation, however, get in the way of a good commercial idea. 'Banana Republic' has more lately been employed as the name of a chain of mid-range clothing stores.

through monopoly control of its market. As for repressive regimes, they were United Fruit's best friends, with coups d'état among its specialities. United Fruit had possibly launched more exercises in 'regime change' on the banana's behalf than had even been carried out in the name of oil.

United Fruit had set the template for capitalism, the first of the modern multi-nationals. Certainly there had been other and older big companies, the British East India Company, for example, which had been at its peak in the 1700s. By the mid-nineteenth century, however, the East India Company, was a licensed agent of the Crown and dependent on the British Empire. United Fruit knew better: it did things differently and beyond formal imperialism. It could often count on the help of the US government and the CIA but maintained its boast that it had 'never called in the marines'.

There were other older companies than United Fruit in the modern era too, but originally they had been stay-at-home types. The US's nineteenth-century 'robber barons' in oil, railways, steel and banking made their profits without straying far beyond national borders. They had paid a penalty for this as eventually laws were made to curb their practices and, to some extent, they were forced to 'behave'. By contrast, for a long time United Fruit had avoided this fate because it was out on a wider frontier. It had set up its own enclave in Central America, a network of far-flung plantations and company towns that acted as an experimental laboratory for capitalism, unhindered, unwatched and forging ahead into the great unknown.

United Fruit had started with a few bananas grown at the side of a railway line and become a global power. It took many forms and went by many names: *La Frutera*, the fruit company; *El Yunay,* as in *Yunay*-ted Fruit; or simply *La Compañía*. Famously it was *El Pulpo*, the octopus, its tentacles everywhere. It was greedy and controlled millions of acres of land, only a relatively small part of which it used. In countries of many landless small farmers, it kept the rest to keep out competitors and for a 'rainy day'. In and around its plantations it had fifteen hundred miles of railways, a good number of which its host countries built and paid for.

United Fruit's Great White Fleet of refrigerated ships, 'reefers', comprised the world's largest private navy. Painted against the heat, its ships ran cruises to places of which people could scarcely dream: Havana with its casinos, brothels and other palaces of entertainment; the cays of Belize; the Panama Canal. Its in-house slogan, however, upheld its status as a merchant line: 'every banana a guest, every passenger a pest'.

Its plantation hospitals, which were mainly built to accommodate its supervisors and managers brought down from the US, formed the largest private health system in the world. In Guatemala the company saved the Mayan ruins of Quiriguá from the jungle. It installed the tramways and electric street lighting of the Costa Rican capital, San José. United Fruit was power.

For my thesis I read the available material on the company. There was a lot of it, more as far as I could tell than on any other company in the modern era. For years United Fruit had attracted a great deal of attention. Myriad articles, academic dissertations and polemics between left and right had been devoted to it. United Fruit had even made the leap into literature, not that it would have chosen to. Pablo Neruda was from Chile, in South America, and well away from United Fruit's sphere of influence, yet in 1950 he felt inspired to include a critique of the company in his epic poem about the Americas, *Canto General.* Through such attention, United Fruit had entered Latin American folklore. García Márquez had illustrated the point in the 1960s. Also, Miguel Ángel Asturias, from Guatemala, had written his novel, *The Green Pope*, about United Fruit's exploits in his country and had won the Nobel Prize for literature in 1967.

By the mid-1970s the hostile debate that United Fruit had long prompted had died down. The company had transformed into being more a matter for cultured reflection than fiery invective. Maybe, I dared to presume, *El Pulpo* wasn't quite the tentacled power it had once been. Then something happened as if itself an act of magical realism. After a sudden, almost violent upsurge of interest in United Fruit around the time of Black's suicide, the company vanished.

The famously moral, late and departed chief of United Fruit hadn't been what he had seemed. He had bribed members of the military government of Honduras. He had calculated that, in their country's hour of need after Hurricane Fifi, a small inducement – one and a quarter million dollars – might encourage them to pull Honduras out of the banana cartel that had waged war on United Fruit.

Historically, this was a very United Fruit thing to do. 'Fruit company bribes Central American militarist' had become over the years less the stuff of news than a statement of the obvious. Yet the transgression provoked a storm of opprobrium, a whirlwind of moral outrage. Strangely enough, this was not from United Fruit's most obvious enemies – bolshie students, academic polemicists and Latin American magic realists – but from its own kind.

Wall Street was outraged. The company's shares crashed. The financial authorities muscled in to seize its books, to prevent 'its further violation of the law'. The cry went up that United

Fruit was up to its old tricks again from quarters willing to overlook them in the past. The effect was to drive United Fruit out of the temple. It was as if a death squad from the company's old Central American area had 'disappeared' it off the streets. United Fruit's anti-democratic tendencies in the past had done much to encourage death squad activities. Now events followed a familiar pattern. Quickly everyone stopped talking about the victim in anything but whispers; soon they did not mention it at all. Had it ever been there?

As for Eli Black, more details emerged on how he had met his end. To smash his office window he had used his briefcase, which was laden with papers and heavy books. He had thrown the briefcase out of the window, the papers scattering for blocks around and retrieved by the postal and emergency workers who had been engaged in the clear-up. One scrap was the nearest anyone found to a suicide note. On it Black had written 'early retirement, 55', suggesting he had plans to leave the company, or others had such plans for him.

It materialised that Black had lost the confidence of his senior managers, who had been trying to get him out of the company and into retirement. As a face-saving measure they had approached the State Department, in its capacity as guardian of the US's foreign and diplomatic affairs, asking if any overseas ambassadorships were up for renewal. The names of a number of countries came back in reply, the most likely of which was Costa Rica. There remains no way of knowing whether Black would have taken the post, or if Costa Rica would have taken someone from United Fruit. But it was the country where United Fruit's story had begun a century before.

In the circularity of his masterwork, it seemed that García

Márquez might have predicted United Fruit's fate. The author had referred to his imaginary Macondo in *One Hundred Years of Solitude* as a 'city of mirrors (or mirages)'. How United Fruit had maintained its rule had been an exercise in smoke and mirrors, a huge confidence trick as practised by a collection of chancers and charlatans, philanthropists and fakirs. Yet, in singular fashion, the United Fruit Company had for a century somehow controlled a vast domain. Finally, the company, like Macondo, had been struck by a biblical hurricane and, with disaster imminent, its last character had engaged in a deranged search for meaning, knowing he was not going to get out of it alive. In its heyday one of the most formidable companies in the world, United Fruit had been 'wiped out by the wind and exiled from the memory of men'.

But exiles can return.

2

Lament for a Dying Fruit

Bananas are cheap and all around us, but they don't grow on trees. With no woody trunk or bough, the banana is a plant, a herb and the world's tallest grass. Rodgers and Hammerstein further confused the issue in *South Pacific* with their evocation of a primitive island paradise and 'bananas you can pick right off a tree'. The fruit does not ripen well when still on the plant and tends to grow sour. It is best picked and shipped when green. Normally bananas come from a plantation in a very distant country to point of sale within twelve to thirteen days, three hundred hours, of cutting. Any later and they start to rot. The vast majority of bananas arrive in good time and see out their last days before market in industrial ripening rooms.

Hot and damp are the banana's preferred conditions for growth, such as those found in the coastal lowlands of the tropics. Central America's Atlantic coast is therefore perfect. Bananas rarely grow outside the tropics. Israel is one exception and Iceland another, in proximity to its steaming geysers. Florida was once tried as a banana location but its occasional frosts proved the experiment's unravelling. Bananas thrive in rich sandy loam and, since they grow in areas where it rains a lot, need good drainage. Banana plants enjoy the ambiance of swamp but not actually being in it; they cannot survive standing in water.

Banana plants grow to a height of between two and a half and nine metres. The taller they are, the more vulnerable they are to hurricanes. To grow them, cuttings are taken from the underground stems of mature plants and planted. A month later a tight roll of leaves appears. As they grow, these rolls unfurl, quite fast, every six to twelve days and look like large drooping feathers. The pulpy, fibrous 'trunk' of the banana plant is really the stalks of these leaves. Full-grown leaves, or fronds, are up to three metres long and sixty centimetres wide and have a certain sweeping elegance, until they split across and start to look untidy.

After ten months a large bud appears from the unrolling leaves, at the end of a stem. The bud itself is made up of small purple leaves that pull back to reveal clusters of small flowers. These clusters grow into tiny banana bunches. Bunches are 'hands', the bananas called 'fingers'. They grow at eight to twenty fingers per hand and five to ten hands per stem. As the stems become heavier, they bend down and droop towards the ground, and as the bananas grow larger they curve upwards.

Four to five months later the fruit is harvested by cutting the stem down. The violated stem gives off a sticky juice. Experienced stem carriers, often known in the trade as 'backers', will wear an appropriate hat to avoid having this juice leak into their hair. I shampooed mine thoroughly every day and bleached it dry in the afternoon sun. It looked great for a while. After a few weeks, my hair fell out.

Bananas grow in distant realms, mysterious places, out of sight and mind. They flourish in areas hostile to man, malarial regions, full of mosquitoes. It is said that if you wipe a mosquito bite with the inside of a banana skin it will ease the itch. I've tried it and it worked for me. We attribute to bananas all sorts of qualities, real and imagined.

Bananas have been said to solve virtually every health problem: obesity, blood pressure, depression, constipation. They have natural sugars for lasting energy, potassium to regulate blood sugar levels, fibre for the bowels. They lift the mood or alternatively calm you down, containing the neurotransmitters dopamine and seratonin that, respectively, replicate Ecstasy and Prozac.

Bananas stand for 'peace and love'. Donovan sang about this in the 1960s in 'Mellow Yellow'. According to his song's lyrics, the banana was capable of 'electrical' effect. To achieve it, the counter-culture smoked the scraped and dried innards of banana skins, or so it was said.

The banana makes us laugh. In a light-hearted way it is associated with insanity: 'going bananas', says the *Oxford English Dictionary*, entered linguistic currency in 1935. Comedy had a great deal of fun with the fruit: Charlie Chaplin and many others slipped on it. From the 1920s to the 1950s music halls ran riot with it: 'Have a banana!' It was perhaps suggestive but difficult to take seriously. Banana humour is of the type featured on 'dirty' postcards of the 1950s sent from outreaches of England's disappeared holiday land like Clacton and Bognor Regis.

In the US Carmen Miranda danced and sang with bananas to great acclaim in her films of the 1930s and 1940s. In one, *The Gang's All Here*, her female chorus laid around her waving huge make-believe bananas between their legs. The scene ended with an explosion of tropical fruit from her tutti-frutti hat.

Bananas speak to our insecurities, male in particular. Are we up to it? United Fruit used to make play of this in its advertising. No banana of less than nine inches, it boasted, was fit for requirements. Of course, the company presented this as pure statement of fact; salacious interpretation would not have been of its doing. With phallic symbolism in mind, manuals on etiquette at the turn of the nineteenth and twentieth centuries taught well-bred American ladies the correct way to eat bananas. On drawing back the skin, this was not by way of direct conveyance to the mouth. Nor was the fruit to be touched by the fingers. A silver knife and fork were used to cut and duly dispatch the banana in bite-sized pieces. Any gentleman in attendance at such a ritual might have had cause to shift uncomfortably in his chair.

The banana manages to mask much of its subliminal side with assumed qualities of innocence. Advertisements in the 1950s and 1960s on British commercial television, still a novel phenomenon at the time, invited you to 'Unzip a Banana'. Was any connection drawn between zipping and zippers? We wouldn't consciously have thought about it. Anyway, fly buttons were still the norm.

In the late 1950s Harry Belafonte had a huge hit with the 'Banana Boat Song', a calypso about stevedores in the Caribbean approaching the end of their night shift: 'Dayy-O!' It all sounded like they were having a great deal of fun. Listening to it in Britain, I had no grasp of why anyone would want to leave such a place. Yet it was already over a decade since in 1948 the *Windrush*, a banana boat, had brought the first shipment of Caribbean migrants seeking work and a new life in England. In 1958 there had been 'race riots' in the Notting Hill district of London with the immigrant community alleged to be 'stealing our jobs' and – perhaps more significantly – 'stealing our women'.

As for the banana's innocence being confounded by coups d'état and other such political machinations in the regions where it is grown, we simply wouldn't have known of such a thing. (Incidentally, no one laughs at the banana in its areas of origin. It is far too serious a business, on which jobs and lives depend. When I worked in Central America, I never heard one banana joke.)

The banana spans our history of imperfection from the fanciful origins of man to the modern consumer society. Scholarly observations on the matter have suggested that it was probably a banana leaf, rather than a fig leaf, that Adam and Eve wore in the Garden of Eden to hide their shame. The fig leaf might have looked most appropriate, but would have been too difficult to attach to the body. The banana leaf, with its superior ability to drape and wrap around things, was far more suited to the part.

When it comes to our contemporary shopping preferences, there are few more popular items than the banana. It has long since outstripped the apple as our favourite fruit. Recent claims have gone further, rating the banana among the most popular products on supermarket shelves. One study, which presumably set aside such dull basics of life as milk and bread, suggested that the only products beating the banana on to our supermarket shopping lists were petrol and lottery tickets. Whether these qualify as true supermarket items may be a moot point, but, either way, what is an exotic and apparently marginal piece of fruit stakes an extraordinary claim on consumer affections.

Clement Attlee, Britain's prime minister in the early years after the Second World War, had a United Fruit shipload of bananas brought over in 1945 to herald the idea of a bright new future. This was to be 'Social Democracy' and the 'welfare state' and the boat had a banana on board for each child and pregnant mother of the land. His gesture, however, was taken in other ways. Evelyn Waugh, the novelist, saw it in more melancholic terms, of a lost and glorious past. When the bananas arrived for his three children, he had his wife serve the fruit with rare cream and sugar and scoffed the lot in front of them. (His son Auberon later wrote that he had not taken anything his father had to say on faith and morals very seriously thereafter.)

The British public at large was less disposed to view the bananas as a gift from a benevolent state than as a promise of greater luxuries to come. They would remain disappointed for some while. Attlee delivered his greatest triumph three years later, the National Health Service, and I was born in the first week of it in an English stately home converted into a hospital. 1948 was the year when Britain's post-war austerity reached a height, along with the public's frustration with it. By then the subversive banana had long since slipped in beneath the wire and people were hankering for more of the TVs, fridges, cars and other goods they heard everyone had in America.

In some areas the banana's weird allure lasted for the duration of the Cold War and beyond. In Eastern Europe bananas became the symbol of 'The West'. Longer queues formed for them in the Soviet Union than for other foods. In East Germany people laid out virtual altars of bananas, keeping them for as long as possible to be looked at or offered to honoured guests. Rare visitors from the West found themselves mystified by the solemn ceremony that accompanied such a seemingly commonplace gift.

When the Berlin Wall came down in 1989 freelance opportunists were first into the breach, relieving East Berliners of their five free Western Deutschmarks in exchange for bananas. The East Berliners didn't care. They bought them, ate them and marched on to the other side. Many sang and chanted as they went: 'Hold my hand, and take me to Banana Land'.

Contrary to its appearance as a primitive thing of nature, the banana we know is nothing of the kind. United Fruit created it. The company took bananas out of their jungle environment – they don't grow particularly well there – and put them into huge plantations, for mass production and mass consumption.

The banana is of the botanical genus *Musa* and has some three hundred varieties. One wild type, *Musa acuminata* is a giant jungle herb containing a mass of hard seeds that make it all but inedible. *Musa paradisiaca* is among the long macho varieties associated with Afro-Caribbean cuisine. Dessert bananas include the stubby Red Macabu and the small yellow Lady Finger. Another type dares to be named 'Apple'. One tastes more like a pear. Bananas come short and long, while some are straight, as if to comply with a mythical regulation of the European Union. Another, the quadrilateral, is square.

United Fruit whittled the varieties for its purposes down to one. This was the Gros Michel or 'Big Mike'. It was economically 'efficient', good for profits. More sizeable than alternative varieties like the Red Macabu or Lady Finger, Big Mike meant consumers simply ate more banana. It also travelled well. With a thicker skin than some, Big Mike arrived at its destination with less bruising.

United Fruit was a pioneer of mass production. With its one-size-fits-all banana, the company beat Henry Ford, the man often credited as the pioneer of industrial standardisation, by a number of years. Big Mike was on the shelves at the turn of the twentieth century; the Model T motor car, on the other hand, rolled off the production line in 1908.

Big Mike also suited the most general of tastes. It was not too big or too small, too yellow, or too sweet. In fact, it was a little bland. After a while no one really knew any different, incapable as they were of remembering any other kind. United Fruit's bananas were the forerunners of those products we know today: the cup of cross-cultural coffee foam; the multinational hamburger. For Big Mike read Big Mac.

Bananas weren't seen in great number in Europe till some way into the first decade of the twentieth century. My grandmother recalled people biting straight into them; they had to be shown how to peel them. Today the British and Americans eat twelve to thirteen kilos, about seventy bananas per person per year. Developing countries mainly consume savoury cooking bananas, a staple of diet. The banana is the world's fourth major food after rice, wheat and milk.

It is thought to have originated in the rainforests of Malaysia in the Stone Age, discovered by cavemen some ten thousand years ago. The name 'banana' comes from Africa. At some time, somehow it jumped continents. Experts rummaging in fossilised rubbish pits in Cameroon have found banana tissue dating back 2,500 years. From West Africa the banana found its way to the Canaries, and thence onward with the Spanish conquest to the Americas.

The entrepreneurial friar Tomás de Berlanga landed with it in 1516 in Hispaniola, the island now divided between the Dominican Republic and Haiti. He ascended Catholicism's corporate ladder to become bishop of Panama and took the banana with him as he moved west across the Caribbean to the Central American mainland.

Early reports in the US had it turning up in Salem, Massachusetts in the 1690s, during the strange period of the witch-hunts. Someone cooked up the fruit with pork and may have decided it tasted like the devil's own food. Bananas disappeared in the north-eastern US till the early nineteenth century when they fetched up again with old sea dogs from the Caribbean as items for sale, or gifts for incredulous relatives and friends.

In 1950s North London we got ours from the Banana Man halfway up Islington's Chapel Market. He was a sad-faced Italian, growling ''ere y'are, getchyer bananas'. The label on each bunch, in white letters against a dark blue background, said 'Fyffes'. I mistakenly took this to be a 'British' company – one of those that were all around us like Woolworth's and Ford. But at that time Fyffes was part of the United Fruit Company.*

The banana's cheeriness looked unconvincing in the grey of smoggy London but it was always there, where seasonal fruits like apples weren't. Soon we took it for granted. If we had thought about it, we would have been aware that it was from the hot countries, and poor ones too. But we would have had no idea the fruit came by way of an intensive process of production, shipping and distribution.

The fact of the matter was that for most of the twentieth century United Fruit had a monopoly on the industry. Today four companies dominate, Chiquita, Del Monte and Dole from the US, and Noboa from Ecuador. A name sometimes

* Today Fyffes is Irish and independent.

given them speaks for the banana industry's 'buccaneering' tradition: the 'Wild Bunch'.

Now the banana itself is disappearing. It is apparently going the way of its creator, United Fruit. In 2003 it emerged that the banana might have only a decade to live. Its main growing regions of the tropics have no seasons as understood in temperate climes. The banana, therefore, is always working and has no downtime. The same applies to the pathogens created for no other reason than to attack it.

Panama disease is what they call a fusarial wilt, a microbe that attacks from beneath at the root of the plant. It cuts off the banana plant's water supply and chokes it to death. Sigatoka is named after a verdant valley in Fiji, where it was first identified, and is a spore that sweeps in on the wind and rain. It attacks the leaves of the plant, removing the protection they afford the fruit, which then ripens prematurely. Black sigatoka has emerged as a nasty variant, while Panama disease has recently derived a new form of its own. No one comes up with colourful names anymore: this one is just called by its laboratory name of 'Tropical Race 4'.

The banana, however, has a deeper weakness. This is genetic. Most bananas on inspection have no seeds to talk of, which, in reproductive terms, is a disaster. The banana does not come to us by the processes of botanical intercourse. The *New Scientist* pointed this out when it broke the news of the banana's pending demise. The banana 'hasn't had sex for thousands of years', said the magazine unkindly. The fruit is effectively a clone, discovered by those Malaysian cavemen and planted from cuttings ever since. Without sexual reproduction to re-combine its genes in new arrangements, the banana has become more vulnerable to disease. This has been made worse by the commercial fixation of producing a single variety everywhere. The banana is ripe for attack from any potential pest since, while its pests are constantly evolving to find ways of carrying out their onslaught, the banana is not evolving at all.

Big Mike succumbed as long ago as the 1950s. Another variety, the Cavendish, was found to replace it and called 'disease resistant' but now faces the same fate. Disease has been a threat for many years, without the public knowing it. Panama disease hit United Fruit's plantations in Panama over a hundred years ago. Sigatoka hit Central America in the 1930s.

United Fruit and its successors have since waged war on the banana's enemies with pesticides and fungicides being pumped onto the fruit at an increasing rate. Of the world's major food crops, the banana is the most chemically treated and we trust a great deal, therefore, to the prophylactic powers of its skin. The chemicals have proved ever less effective for the task assigned them, however, and the revelation in 2003 of the banana's crisis came when it finally seemed to dawn on the companies that they had run out of ideas.

For many years they had left the banana-producing countries, with their scant resources, to seek alternative solutions themselves. Scientists skilled in genetic modification have now been hired in an effort to clone in some factor – to discover the mysterious combinations – that might save the fruit.

But, as they graft and clone, so the banana is dying, and a process that might have occurred anyway over the centuries has been greatly accelerated by United Fruit and its kind. It took the fruit out of the jungle and turned a natural product into a 'commodity', a thing of commerce and the mass market. As a result it appears unequal to the business of survival.

United Fruit's own demise seemed to precede what may well be that of the product it gave us by some thirty to forty years. According to most accounts, the business practices that United Fruit was synonymous with have been consigned to the historical dustbin. Lately, however, the signs are of the old company's re-emergence as a model for the corporate world. The spirit it championed has been revamped and presented to us as the miracle formula by which we are required to live in the era of globalisation.

The whole business of United Fruit began, by chance, one hundred and forty years ago.

3

Roots of Empire

Chief justice of the Supreme Court of Costa Rica, Dr José María Castro rose to his feet at midday on August 18, 1871 to make his speech. A collection of the nation's dignitaries was gathered behind him on the large wooden podium: the archbishop of San José, from the country's capital fifteen miles away to the east; the large coffee growers, still sizing up what this day would signify for them; Doña Pacífica Fernández de Castro, the speaker's wife and designer of the national flag, was also present, along with several of their fifteen children. Seated next to her was the guest of honour, General Tomás Guardia, the new president. He had seized power the year before, proclaiming that he would 'break the oligarchy' and 'establish democracy'. To achieve this Costa Rica needed to be connected to the world.

Castro had twice been president of the republic and twice deposed by the army. The coffee oligarchs who controlled the wealth of the country regularly got together with the military to impose or depose presidents as they wished. General Guardia had recently taken over, vowing that this would not happen again. It was the reason Costa Rica was getting the railway.

The railroad would run from the small town of Alajuela, at the western end of the mesa, Costa Rica's high upland plateau. It would proceed east for 100 miles down to the Atlantic coast. Generally no one went there. The flag that

Doña Pacífica had designed – now strung from balconies and lampposts in Alajuela's tiny streets and town square in the breeze of an immaculately clear Costa Rican day – showed the nation's problem: at the banner's centre was a broad horizontal stripe in red, for the sun that warmed the mesa on which nearly all Costa Ricans lived. The white bands around it were for the mid-afternoon clouds that brought the rain to irrigate its rich volcanic soil. The blue stripes at the outer edges represented Costa Rica's Pacific and Atlantic coasts.

The Pacific was fine: it had a port. From there, Costa Rica's coffee went out to the world. The trouble was that both the coffee and any wealthy Costa Ricans bound for the east coast of the United States and Europe had to sail around the perilous Cape Horn. The journey, if completed, took months. The only alternative was the railroad across Panama, built by the US for the gold rush in the 1850s and its ramshackle carriages still full of the roughnecks that followed in its path.

In 1502, on his fourth voyage, Columbus had landed on the Atlantic coast and called it 'Costa Rica', the 'rich coast'. It was an act of wishful thinking. He had to report back to his patrons at home, to whom he had oversold the goods on offer; 'lands of vanity and delusion' they were calling them. Columbus left Costa Rica for the most miserable stage of his voyages yet, his fleet tramping the coast in northerly storms looking for what he imagined might be a sea passage through to China. He turned for home racked with arthritis and with his ships being eaten by seaworms.

Costa Rica's large Atlantic province of Limón remained mostly uninhabited but that, as Castro assured his audience, would soon change. Twelve thousand people had packed into

Alajuela, one in twelve of the nation's population, and they listened as he mapped out the future. Fifty years on from independence from Spain, the swamp and desolation of Limón would succumb to the force of progress.

The task had been assigned to the finest in the business. This was Henry 'Don Enrique' Meiggs, the great American railway builder, presently resident in Peru. The contracts had been signed and the pledges made: the railway would be finished in three years. At which point, and by the grace of God and General Guardia, Costa Ricans would be led down from their mountain to the sea.

After the cheers, the archbishop gave the Te Deum. Guardia descended from the podium to turn the project's first clod of earth with a silver shovel, specially cast. It started to rain, a little earlier than normal. After siesta the crowds took to the streets again with itinerant bands of acrobats and musicians. The parties, and a ball for the VIPs, went on until five the following morning.

Those placed in charge of the works had not yet arrived. Henry Keith, thirty-two, and his younger brother by nine years, Minor, were still at sea. They had taken a steamer south from New York and at Panama would cross the Central American isthmus on the railway built for the gold rush. On the Pacific side they took a ship north to Costa Rica and arrived on the mesa three weeks after the official opening of the works on the railway, 'at the trot of their horses'.

Through them, 'Don Enrique' Meiggs, their uncle, conveyed his regrets. He wouldn't have time to construct Costa Rica's railway since he was otherwise engaged. He was building Peru's line from Lima up into the Andes, a bigger and far trickier project. His nephews, however, came with all the necessary skills for the task at hand and as part of the family firm. He thoroughly recommended them.

For all the prowess ascribed to him as an engineer, Meiggs was principally a talented political fixer and, when he was caught out, a crook. From Brooklyn, he had followed the gold rush and made a fortune from land speculation on the San Francisco waterfront. Accused of theft of city funds and stock market fraud, he later fled to South America. He made more millions from building the coastal railways of Chile and Peru before spotting a greater opportunity in the guano deposits, a key source of agricultural fertiliser, of Peru's offshore Chincha Islands. Estimates of his fortune from this slippery enterprise went as high as five hundred million dollars; this was incredible for the day and, if true, put Meiggs halfway to being a birdshit billionaire. He employed some of his monetary reserves vetting membership of the governments of Peru, Chile and Bolivia, and arranging tax rates to his advantage.

Henry Keith had been with his uncle in Peru at the time the deal was struck and had assured the Costa Ricans that he knew the area where their railway was to be. Every construction company of any worth was interested in building a canal across Central America. Panama was one possible location for it, but the favoured candidate was the San Juan River dividing Costa Rica and Nicaragua on their Atlantic coasts. Henry Keith had been there, he said, and had surveyed the Limón seaboard. He understood whatever hazards it might have in store. On that basis, Costa Rica's railway would take three years to complete.

The Keiths were from Brooklyn, their father a wealthy lumber merchant. They were Scottish some generations back; family tales had them on eleventh-century nodding terms with

King Malcolm II. Allegedly they had had some claim to royal title and land in the region of East Lothian. The Meiggs side of the family claimed English background and to have emigrated from the southern county of Dorset in 1635.

The junior of the two, Minor Cooper Keith had not settled to anything. An expensive education saw him take up a position in menswear in a Broadway store at three dollars a week. He went into wood with his father, who then – having bought Padre Island, a hundred-mile sandbar off the Texas coast – sent Minor to run it as a ranch. Surrounded by a lot of water, wildfowl and deer, Minor enjoyed the solitude but not a great deal of luck. Market prices were not what he had hoped for. A hurricane off the Gulf of Mexico also blew a thousand of his cows into the sea. When his brother Henry wrote to him saying he could make more money in Costa Rica in three years than on Padre in a lifetime, he was easily persuaded. With so many in search of El Dorado, Minor took off in pursuit of his.

Older brother Henry took the easy part of the work, on the mesa. A locomotive was on rails and running around Alajuela within weeks, scaring the people; 'they thought to hell it would take them', said a report of the engine that spat steam and fire. Henry named it the 'Limón Number One'.

Minor was packed off to Limón with mules and a guide. 'Dreary miles of uninhabited beach', read one description of the scene that greeted him, 'but for the huts of a few Caribs and other Indians'. There was no fresh meat or vegetables. Stretching away into the unremitting heat lay the 'interminable swamp'.

Minor Keith's job was to run the workforce. He was to hire it and sell it things from the commissary, the company store: clothing, basic provisions and machetes for hand-to-hand combat with the jungle. He had some banana cuttings that he had picked up on his way to Costa Rica while passing through Panama. He planted them. The fruit would grow quite quickly and he could sell it to the men.

Some Jamaicans had already been hired to clear the jungle and swamp but Minor wanted hardened US labour. He took the project's steamboat to New Orleans to recruit from its waterfront bars and flophouses. At a dollar a day and food, many occupants of the city's jail were also keen to offer their services. As they lined up on the dockside ready to embark, the police chief couldn't believe his luck in getting rid of them.

Keith's recruits included a good number of US Civil War veterans. Some even had tropical experience of a kind. The latter had been William Walker's men. Walker was another Scots emigré and had come to the US in the 1840s. He had also set off to chance his luck in Central America. His methods of extending the US frontier were more Old World than New and in the 1850s he had declared himself King of Nicaragua. The US government in Washington, enamoured of this regal idea, gave him its support.

His mistake was to make an enemy of Cornelius Vanderbilt, the US railway and shipping magnate who had established a presence in the area with the intention of building the trans-isthmian canal. When Walker fired on Vanderbilt's boats on the San Juan River between Nicaragua and Costa Rica, Vanderbilt hired Central American mercenaries to retaliate. Walker fled for the US aboard an American gunboat. He later returned to pronounce himself king again, though he only made it as far as Nicaragua's northern neighbour, Honduras. Here in 1860 he was put against a wall and shot.

Many of Keith's new employees jumped ship in Havana, the first port of call made to take on sugar. When the boat ran aground on the Chinchorro Bank in a night storm off Yucatán, Keith and a few loyalists had to hold off the rest at gunpoint from rushing the lifeboats. Only when the storm eased next day were the malcontents persuaded to help jettison cargo and re-float the boat.

All but a few of this shipment and others that followed died working in Limón. No proper records were kept but the first twenty-five miles of the Costa Rican railway were estimated to have cost four thousand lives. Malaria and yellow fever were the main causes, though no one at the time knew of the part played by the Atlantic coast's especially virulent mosquitoes. Word went around among New Orleans' dwindling supply of labour that Keith was an employer to avoid. He was obliged to turn almost exclusively to recruiting Jamaicans.

The railway advanced only four miles in the first year. No proper survey had been done. The money ran out thanks to mishandled bond issues in London. With the Civil War only just behind it, the US was no good for credit. The Franco–Prussian war had put Europe's continental bankers out of commission and the bankers in London saw the Keiths and the Costa Ricans coming. Most of the loans raised went in interest payments.

In 1873 the markets crashed. Henry Keith went home claiming Costa Rica owed him money and calling for US intervention. Still engaged in its period of post-Civil War reconstruction, Washington confined its action to a letter of polite enquiry. Henry returned to Costa Rica only to join the multitude struck down by disease. He died leaving both the railway and his younger brother Minor stranded.

★ ★ ★

Pride of official place in 1876 at the Great Centennial Exhibition in Philadelphia went to George H. Corliss's magnificent contraption. The Rhode Island engineer's steam engine rose like the nation itself: 'not a superfluous ounce of metal on it', wrote William Dean Howells, the novelist and editor of Boston's *Atlantic Monthly* magazine. Its 56-ton flywheel whirred 'with a hoarded power that makes all tremble'. In fact it did not hoard its power but supplied it free to other exhibitors, if not on every day. The exhibition closed on Sundays, when Corliss would not allow his machine to be used.

Ten years after the end of the Civil War, the exhibition's principal intention was to announce the US's arrival among the industrial élite of nations. Its sixty-seven buildings spread across a square kilometre, the expanse of two hundred American football fields. Staged from May to November, it attracted eight million people in a country of forty-six million: 'sleek, confident and well-fed'. Most worked ten hours a day, six days a week, and with no paid time off. Many took unpaid leave to visit.

Entry cost was fifty cents, the average worker's daily wage a dollar twenty-one. The gates took five million dollars, one thousand and one of them counterfeit. Of the five hundred and four children lost, all but five were returned to their families the same day, the rest the next. Four people died, none from foul play. There were six hundred and seventy-five arrests, fourteen of which were for pick-pocketing. One person was also arrested for fornication, though with no indication as to with whom.

'The American invents as the Greeks sculpted and the Italians painted,' wrote *The Times* of London, worried about Britain's loss of technological supremacy. Scotsman Alexander Graham Bell, lately of Boston, displayed his newly invented telephone.

Thomas Edison presented his telegraph. The typewriter was seen for the first time, as was the Otis brothers' steam elevator machine. George Eastman, twenty-two, wrote home to his mother in Rochester, New York, that he intended to 'traverse every aisle'. No mean feat; this amounted to eleven miles in the main exhibition hall alone. Eastman was five years from perfecting his easy-to-carry camera with flexible rolled film.

The Line-Wolf ammonia compressor represented an important advance in the technology of man-made ice. Also on show was a new refrigerated type of railroad car for perishable freight. James Tufts, a Massachusetts entrepreneur, exhibited his soda fountain, which in a dozen years or so would be usefully employed by Coca-Cola.

Exhibits from overseas were held to be of poor calibre, save that from France, a sister republic and close historical friend. France sent the first completed part of the Statue of Liberty, the right arm and torch. Fifty feet high, it put other foreign offerings in the shade. Turkey sent a scarf dancer. Germany sent a few machines courtesy of Krupp, the German ambassador complaining they did nothing to brighten the dull image of Prussia. Japan, noted William Dean Howells, sent an exhibit of arts and crafts manned by a 'small lady-handed carpenter' who 'now and then darted a disgusted look through his narrow eye-slits at the observer'.

The Centennial organisers had planned an ethnology section to feature Native Americans. The Department of the Interior objected. The organisers offered to use only the 'cleanest and finest looking', who would be English-speaking and accompanied by a child, dog and pony. Their idea was rejected and they had to use life-sized plaster models. Even this was too much for Howells. In the 'extermination of the red savage', he wrote, 'one could hardly regret the loss of any number of Apaches and Comanches'. And he wrote this before word filtered through at the end of June of the massacre of Colonel George Custer and two hundred cavalrymen at Little Big Horn River.

The news from the South Dakota Territory almost ruined the republic's one-hundredth birthday party on July 4. The fact was, however, that the frontier was all but tamed. The US's transcontinental railway had been completed in 1869. Barbed wire, invented in 1873, contained the vast expanses between east and west. Out in the western mountains, Colorado became the thirty-eighth state of the Union during the exhibition.

The Centennial Exhibition's message was of a thrusting, forward-looking nation. Some popular events played to the idea of the US as pre-industrial idyll: the Strawberry Display, the Trial of Reaping Machines, the Exhibit of Sheep, Swine and Goats. But the flat stoneless plains of the Midwest had long since been transformed into the nation's grain basket. It was forty-five years since Cyrus McCormick had invented his revolutionary reaper. Or had he stolen the idea from the Virginian slave who helped him construct it? The reaper had featured over the years in several grim courtroom battles. For one of them McCormick had engaged Abraham Lincoln, a young Illinois lawyer.

By the time of the Centennial Exhibition the question was being asked whether the US's age of invention wasn't also one of blatant manipulation. Market crashes ran at a rate of one a decade. The 'small man' always ended up ruined. The crash of 1873 had seen President Ulysses S. Grant, the Civil War leader and hero accused of accepting gifts from businessmen. The robber barons were blamed, characters like Vanderbilt, Jay Gould, Daniel Drew and James Fisk. Their preferred title was 'captains of industry'. Gould and Fisk had attempted to buy all the gold in New York City and almost got away with it. The press called Gould the most hated man in America. Drew chimed in that the US had become too democratic.

A hothouse of activity, where was the US to expel its spare energy? For most of the past hundred years, it had turned its back on the Old World, got on with inward development and expanded to its west. But the US had also sketched out a broader frontier. The Monroe Doctrine of 1823 had thrown a boundary rope around the Americas, a 'Keep Out' sign to foreigners. Outside influences remained – colonial vestiges like Spain in Cuba and Britain in Jamaica and other Caribbean islands – but their power had diminished.

Lately there had been a demand for the US's services within the region. In 1869 the government of the Dominican Republic had called for help and, in a parlous financial state, offered to sell itself to the US. President Grant had drawn up a treaty of annexation. The notion was dropped, however, after complaints within the US that it was wrong for a Caribbean republic with a large black population to turn its independence over to the US, especially so soon after the Civil War.

The Centennial Exhibition's most beautiful building was the horticultural hall. In glass and steel, it was of twelfth-century Moresque style with surrounding pools and flowerbeds, a 'reflection of the Victorian passion for nature'. *Leslie's*, the popular magazine, remarked that it was the displays of exotic – even weird – natural phenomena that visitors considered the best part of the exhibition. The horticultural hall also had the advantage of being a compact and manageable area. Walking it amounted to little more than a kilometre. Visitors flocked to view its orchids, orange trees, date palms, fig trees and pineapples, but one item drew special attention: 'a scrubby banana tree', as observed by Frederick Upham Adams, a visitor who in his teens had travelled with his father from distant Illinois.

It stood three and half metres high and a guard had to be mounted to stop the crowds pulling it apart. They would have plucked its fruit 'a diminutive bunch of bananas' – stripped it of its 'bark' and made off with its roots, even the earth it stood in. Apparently they endorsed Adams's view, recorded in a book he wrote nearly forty years later that it was the 'most romantic of all the innumerable things I had seen in any of the (Centennial's) vast buildings'. He had only seen bananas before pictured in geography and religious textbooks, with 'fortunate natives who had nothing to do but roam flowery glades and live on them'. Boa constrictors hung around eating the less fortunate.

Adams's father had worked in Central America and the West Indies and talked often of bananas and other fruits of those 'fever-stricken districts'. In the horticultural hall he held forth again and the frankly curious US crowd gathered round. Most came from distant parts of the world – or had parents who did – but they knew little of it. Here was a hint of what was out there. Adams's father expounded on the difference between this straggly product and its far more bountiful counterpart that grew in the 'warm and humid coastlands near the equator'.

That evening the Adamses walked through the business district of Philadelphia and stopped at a store to buy peaches. Instead they saw a basket of small, cylindrical objects wrapped in tin foil. 'Bananas, a great luxury, sir,' said the shopkeeper. 'This is the only place in Philadelphia which handles them.' They were ten cents each, or six for a half dollar: 'Can I wrap some for you, sir?'

The price was 'more than the native who raised them could earn in a month', said Adams's father but he took a half dozen. Back in the hotel room, the first banana the boy unwrapped was black. This wasn't perfect but it was a banana nonetheless. He had been 'about to bite the skin' when his father stopped him and showed him how to peel it.

Two of the six bananas were too decayed. All were small, three equalling the bulk of one on the market stalls of later years. Adams took the skins home to the Midwest but they were all black and his school friends were unimpressed.

William Dean Howells was, true to form, yet more sceptical. He departed for Boston assessing what he had seen in the horticultural hall as poor fare to the 'unbotanised' eye. His eyes had wearied of palms, cactuses and 'unattainable bananas'.

Other contractors had come in to build the Costa Rican railroad in dribs and drabs. Minor Keith had stayed on, running the company store and the workers. He had planted more bananas in cleared areas by the side of the line but wasn't selling as many as he had hoped: the Jamaicans had started to grow their own.

Fortunately for Keith, a market had stirred elsewhere. In 1870 a schooner captain, Lorenzo Baker from Cape Cod, Massachusetts, had dropped off US gold seekers some way up the Orinoco. From Venezuela he returned via Jamaica looking for cargoes. He had imagined sugar, rum and coconuts but on the quayside at Port Morant he found bananas.

He had seen them before, although many of those that turned up sporadically in the US were of the type known around marketplaces as 'Cuban Reds'. These that Baker saw now were of a yellow variety, more or less green on the stem. He bought them for a few pence and sold at such profit eleven days later in Jersey City that he made further trips. On some, the vagaries of wind and tide told against him and he had to dump his rotting cargo at sea. Baker needed investment, specifically a faster boat. He joined forces with Andrew Preston, a produce buyer in his mid-twenties from Boston. In 1871 they landed their first full shipment of 'Jamaica Yellows' at the city's Long Wharf.

Minor Keith went into business with Gustav Frank, a grower from Panama from whom Keith had picked up the banana cuttings as, in 1871, he first passed through Panama on his way to Costa Rica. Frank was a naturalised American and a former steward on Vanderbilt's Pacific Mail steamships. After the Civil War he began bringing back stems from the Caribbean to the US but since then he had set up small plantations on the Atlantic coast of Panama. Keith sent the railway project's boat to pick up modest shipments from Panama and take them to New Orleans.

Keith also shipped sarsa, vanilla and turtle shell from further north up the coast at a trading post he had established in the rudimentary port of Bluefields, Nicaragua. Up and down the Central American Atlantic seaboard, this was old pirate country. Sir Francis Drake was buried at sea off Panama in Portobelo Bay – 'Capten, art tha sleepin' there below?'* As much English was spoken as Spanish: Puerto Cabezas in Nicaragua was once Bragman's Bluff. From the presence of Miskito Indians, part of the region had acquired its name of the Mosquito Coast. Remote from the capitals of each country, the Atlantic area had seen a new influx of buccaneering foreigners, many from the US enjoying the lack of extradition laws.

* 'Drake's Drum', Sir Henry Newbolt (1862–1938)

But by the end of the 1870s Keith was on the point of returning home. A Caribbean storm had swept away his offshore turtle farm. He remained in charge of labour but the railway's money had again run out and its last contractor departed. Keith faced the prospect of returning to Brooklyn the failed prodigal, unable to run a railway, a ranch or a corral of turtles. Instead President Guardia approached him, in some state of desperation of his own. He suggested Keith might have some success yet: why not take over building the railroad completely?

Keith seized the moment. He said he would need more land, a lot of it. The railroad required freight to survive and bananas for export fitted the bill. Keith went into partnership with a London shipping line and Guardia gave him a million dollars from the national exchequer. Having done so, the Costa Rican leader promptly died in 1882.

Elsewhere other factors worked to Keith's advantage. In science, in the early 1880s, Robert Koch in Germany worked out that germs caused disease. Joseph Lister in Britain and Louis Pasteur in France backed his theory. Cleanliness became the thing and in the US domestic science boomed. Wives and mothers took responsibility for family health risks caused by food or facilities enjoyed by the better-off, like indoor bathrooms. The fast growth in newspapers and magazines encouraged debate about the hitherto neglected subject of 'diet'. More people were literate and read about it. Prior authorities on the subject had once decreed that fresh fruits were liable to 'disarrange the digestive organs'. Now they were 'necessary to perfect health'.

Industrialisation increased rapidly – New York City now had over a million people. The growing middle class used food to define itself, imitating the rich and rejecting the food of the poor. It dumped bluff basics like pork, brown bread, thick soups and dried-fruit pies for more delicate fare. Bananas edged into the profile. They had tropical cachet. Other fruits, like apples, were home grown and the poor could get them easily.

At the same time, more industry meant more working-class people. The cities of New York and Pennsylvania states and the mill towns of New England had populations with that little extra to spend. Life had been hand to mouth but there was now space for some small luxury to lift the mood. Bananas were still thought of as a luxury but they were arriving in number and their price was going down.

In Costa Rica, Guardia's death had left the country without a strongman and with Keith in a key position. He controlled two industries on which the nation's future depended. The railway pushed on into the interior and the verdant valleys of the rivers Matina and Zent. From any hill Keith could survey the terrain before him. He offered to take it off the nation's hands. The Costa Ricans were only too happy and granted him more land than he could possibly use. He set about creating enormous plantations.

The country also handed him control of its finances, or at least that vital part that related to the outside world. The railway still needed loans to fund it and Keith made ready to depart for London to renegotiate Costa Rica's overseas debt.

One other task remained. At thirty-five and suddenly of boundless means, Keith was engaged to a member of the Costa Rican aristocracy. Cristina Castro Fernández was the twelfth child of Dr José María Castro and his wife Doña Pacífica. In keeping with her background, Cristina was of 'good education', which was as well since the burden of communication was mainly hers. After twelve years in Costa Rica, Keith still spoke only minimal Spanish, and it would never really improve.

In 1883 their wedding took place, in Brooklyn. The couple viewed the area's bridge, which had been recently opened and acclaimed as the eighth wonder of the world. Minor Keith had broader horizons. He sailed off to London with his new wife, whose father was twice president of Costa Rica and whose mother had designed the national flag.

4
Monopoly

By 1885 Captain Lorenzo Baker was shipping as many bananas to Boston as he could. He now had bigger and faster ships, eleven all told, on the Caribbean run from Jamaica, Cuba and the Dominican Republic. He named them the Great White Fleet – *La Gran Flota Blanca.*

Andrew Preston, the Boston importer, was taking more orders than Baker could fill. He despatched bananas along the north-east coast of the US and inland in new refrigerated railway cars. Running things from Boston, Preston effectively took control of the show. He banded a group of prominent city names together to form the Boston Fruit Company. Captain Baker was happy to settle in the Caribbean to manage matters from that end.

As it neared completion, the Costa Rican railroad was threatened with ruin because of developments to the south in Panama. The Frenchman Ferdinand de Lesseps began works on a waterway across Panama, after his success building the Suez Canal in Egypt. De Lesseps offered wages of five dollars a day, five times the rate paid by Keith, and Keith's Jamaican workers departed en masse.

Keith found no replacements to his satisfaction elsewhere in the Caribbean and hatched the peculiar plan of getting his labour from northern Italy. In 1887 he hired two thousand workers from Piedmont. They never settled and downed picks and shovels one day in Costa Rica's first known labour strike.

Some went on a protest march to San José. Many absconded into the jungle; about sixty drowned in the mangroves. Keith's later chroniclers reached for some trusty explanations: the Italians had brought their 'secret societies' and 'feuding between family and villages' with them. But how Keith imagined a workforce from the foot of the Alps would toil productively in the hot lowlands of Limón was difficult to fathom.

He was saved by the quick bankruptcy of de Lesseps' Panama canal project. It left hundreds of Jamaicans to fend for themselves in the hills. Keith sent boats down to pick up his errant charges.

Costa Rica's railway pushed to completion sixteen years late in 1890, by which time Keith's status had risen from struggling storekeeper to living legend. Blond, blue-eyed, of medium height and slim, he strode about urging his men on. Stories had them so enamoured of their leader that when the money ran short they went without pay to see the project through. In the work camps he drank copious quantities of cheap whisky with them, the only 'medicines' thought effective against the rigours of the swamp. While the railroad claimed thousands of lives, Keith endured fevers but 'never took a day off sick'. He had plunged headlong into the tide of the Reventazón, Costa Rica's tempestuous principal river, in a sadly vain effort to save a monk on horseback; he barely survived when a bridge he was on collapsed into the torrent. At the end, the driver of the first train to cross the bridge over the Reventazón's last unconquered canyon refused the task, till Keith went ahead. He rode the cowcatcher, the Stars and Stripes cradled in his arms – according, at least, to a painting of the occasion.

Bananas were arriving at such a rate in the US as to prompt a sharp change in their own status. Once bourgeois, the banana was now positively proletarian. Accordingly, magazines advanced the nutritious case for bananas and not just in relation to other fruits. They urged the hard-pressed mother struggling to feed her family to regard the banana as a meat substitute.

The crash of 1893 saw four million thrown out of their jobs. President Grover Cleveland was in the White House, a man with a solid reputation for work. He even answered his own phone. Some of those who got through to him, however, left much to be desired. He arranged to bolster the nation's dwindling reserves through a loan from J. P. Morgan, the bankers. Cleveland's critics denounced him for 'betraying the nation' to the big moneymen of the east.

The debate had moved on a little since the recent times when the robber barons had been defined as the problem. It was now a little less personal, more institutional, and dangerously so. Once, Messrs Morgan, Rockefeller, Gould and others were imagined to rise each morning determined to do mankind down. Some of their number may well have done so. But lately there was a sense that something thrown up by 'the system' was at fault: the large banks and companies. They were known as 'trusts', from a term the economics profession used to denote large industrial and financial monopolies.

Their very name showed how devious they, or indeed economics, could be. The feeling was that they could be 'trusted' above all to feather their own corporate nests. Consequently, Washington introduced the Sherman Anti-Trust Act of 1890 and more legislation soon followed. Initially the laws were to prohibit conspiracies between companies; the setting up of cartels and the like, that led to price fixing and other monopolistic practices.

According to 'natural law', this legislation shouldn't have been necessary. The market, Adam Smith's 'hidden hand', always intervened to rectify wrongdoing. Admittedly, this was never set to happen at any time its supporters could predict and thereby bring some hope to the suffering: the masses of unemployed, for example, that sprung into being with every market crash. But now, with this 'anti-trust' thinking, there was an artificial layer being built into the capitalist system that went against the very spirit of enterprise. It spawned a new breed, the 'regulators' who presumed to oversee the market. They claimed to be as capitalist as those they were created to supervise, who, however, regarded them only as 'sell-outs', a hyena class appointed to tidy up the jungle but really only scavenging for their own benefit.

Keith was at least keeping the flame burning in the jungle proper, out on the system's periphery where the pure spirit of capitalism could flourish in line with the forces of nature. Keith moved into outlying reaches of Colombia, buying extensive banana land near the city of Santa Marta, on the Caribbean coast. Founded in 1525, Santa Marta was one of Spain's oldest settlements in South America and the point from which adventurers anciently set off inland in search of El Dorado. Keith had struck a rich seam in coming across a ready-made asset. Colombian businessmen had developed the Santa Marta banana zone, even constructing their own railroads, but lacked the contacts to build up an international market. As such, they had not been able to compete with the likes of Preston and Keith. Cuckoo-like, Keith now moved into a nest built by others.

Colombia's rulers were quite content to see Keith take over the abandoned northern lands. In the Andean capital, Bogotá, loftily distant from the Caribbean, Colombian governments were historically apt to neglect their far-flung provinces. In 1897, Keith's next gambit was to move into another one – Panama – technically under Colombian rule but yet more remote from Bogotá. Keith's purchase was just across the Panamanian border from his plantations in Costa Rica, a disputed frontier. There was no argument, however, about who was the new and true power in the vicinity.

Keith bought several thousand acres in the Bocas del Toro area of Panama, around Almirante Bay and the Chiriquí Lagoon. It produced more bananas than Costa Rica but Keith's new rivals were small growers – many had begun after losing their jobs on de Lesseps' defunct Panama Canal. Before long he would set about introducing them to the forces of economic rationalisation: namely taking them over.

Keith's ventures into Colombia and Panama were made through his excellent contacts in London. He had made further trips on behalf of Costa Rica's debt problems, while fixing his own beneficial deals. When he was out in the man's world of the City of London, however, life was far lonelier for Mrs Keith than back home with her large Costa Rican family. On one occasion she was found unconscious at the bottom of a lift shaft at the hotel where they were staying in the Maida Vale area of London. Unnoticed for several hours, she survived what may have been a suicide attempt.

Soon Keith established an informal partnership with Andrew Preston's Boston Fruit Company. Boston Fruit's Caribbean lands were unable to meet the burgeoning demand for bananas in the northern US. Keith's Central American plantations supplied the American South through New Orleans and other Gulf of

Mexico ports, with plenty to spare. He sent the surplus to Preston as required.

With an eye on the new anti-trust laws, the new partners quietly agreed not to sell independently in each other's area. Effectively they carved up the US market between them. They drew the line at Cape Hatteras, North Carolina, place of storms and 'graveyard of the Atlantic'. But with their arrangement, Keith and Preston ensured themselves smooth passage into the future. The regulatory hyenas were conspicuous by the absence of their yelping. They were more concerned with the big companies involved in railways, steel, oil and banking whose operations were more domestic and readily visible.

Where Keith almost came unstuck was in the inadvertent backwash of the anti-trust laws. The legislation said companies couldn't conspire and plot together but made no mention of them taking each other over. The result was the great merger wave of the 1890s. Keith had almost survived the difficult years following the 1893 crash in a state of rising prosperity when a company that handled his bananas in New Orleans went bust leaving him with large debts and vulnerable to takeover.

Costa Rica rallied on his behalf, voting large sums of money from the national coffers for Keith to pay off his bankers. Experts on the Costa Rican constitution supposed this was illegal but no one really checked and so another step was taken in the direction of banana republicanism. While Costa Rica's help put him back in the black, it didn't end Keith's troubles. He lacked the cash to run his day-to-day business.

Around the New Orleans waterfront the merger wave had witnessed the number of companies engaged in the banana trade shrink in the past year from a hundred smaller ones to a dozen that were far larger. Keith was a most desirable target for them. Pre-emptively, he approached Preston, a deal of his own in mind.

The new United Fruit Company was a brooding presence across six lands: Costa Rica, Panama, Colombia, Cuba, Jamaica and the Dominican Republic. From the Mosquito Coast, once a haunt of Blackbeard and Morgan, it stretched to the Dominican capital, Santo Domingo in whose cathedral Drake slung his hammock while his men sacked the city in 1587.

It was a giant farm of a little less than two hundred and fifty thousand acres, or a thousand square kilometres. Only a third of the land was tilled. United Fruit would always prefer to hoard much of its energy, partly as a hedge against some future adversity. At the same time, the company figured that if the land were in its hands, then it couldn't be in those of its rivals. At present, this was entirely academic because the new company faced no real competition. United Fruit controlled three quarters of the banana market.

A quiet announcement – one inch square in the press – marked the company's birth on March 30, 1899. Again this reflected a corporate preference: to be understated. Preston would be president of the new giant, Keith its vice-president. This might have been taken to reflect that Keith had come to Preston, cap in hand, to fend off unfriendly takeover. But their need was mutual. In Jamaica, the island's fabled high winds had brought recent destruction to Preston's plantations. The Caribbean islands were relatively contained finite territories, vulnerable possibly to one hurricane wiping out the lot. Central America had its expanses of jungle, thought infinite at the time.

Their job titles also spoke for different aspirations. Keith was the railwayman, rarely happier than when alone in the tropical forest. He now envisioned a Central America 'united by steel', a railway from the borders of Mexico to Panama. On merger, he saw further possibilities and set off across the Caribbean Sea to upgrade Preston's railways in eastern Cuba.

Socially ambitious Preston preferred to stay at home. Boston's 'Brahmins' were a tight-knit bunch that ruled the city and whose number Preston hoped to join. They went back many generations. 'Wasps' – white Anglo-Saxon Protestants – they were mostly of English background, although one leading family, the Cabots, came in 1700 from Jersey in the Channel Islands. Many of the families traced their fortunes to the slave trade, some to the forays of old sea captains to the East Indies. Others had stayed nearer-by, trawling the Grand Banks of Newfoundland. The 'Codfish Aristocracy' was one Brahmin generic. The Lowells had a Massachusetts mill town named after them, the Peabodys helped house the London poor. The families married well and famously, and set up dynasties: the Jefferson Coolidges, the Cabot Lodges. As such they ran the political, economic and social life of a city known as 'Beantown' for one of its favourite foods and the 'Hub' from an assumed central position in the universe. As a local toast would have it: 'And this is good old Boston, The land of the bean and the cod, Where the Lowells talk to the Cabots, And the Cabots talk only to God.'

Little did he suspect, but Preston had missed the boat. He had many now ploughing the seas but Boston's best had quietly closed the gates to further admittance a few years after the Civil War. 'Merchants' weren't what they had been – according to Dr Johnson's definition, he who 'trafficks to remote countries' – but were now 'general traders' and probably too crassly on the make. Preston was the 'right' type who had come in the 'wrong' era.

But that didn't prevent Boston's 'old money' spotting a good financial thing when they saw one, and they backed Preston's business venture. And whatever he lacked in terms of the Brahmins' celestial connections, Preston always had Keith with his feel for the soil. It had been Keith's move to 'plant big' and create enormous plantations. Progressively these featured Big Mike bananas and through the 1890s the bigger pale-skinned variety drove out the Red Macabu, and any other would-be occupants of market terrain. Articles appeared in the press saying how consumers preferred it but consumers took what they got. Long before their time, Keith and Preston had an instinctive grasp of the forces involved. The world of business and economics believed, and for many years yet would continue to do so, that consumer demand somehow just arose. But, wrote Samuel Crowther admiringly, looking back nearly twenty years later on these early days of United Fruit in his book *The Romance and Rise of the American Tropics*, what was being discovered was that 'demand is a thing which must be created'.

Frederick Upham Adams, who as a young boy had been fascinated by the 'scrubby' banana plant at the Philadelphia Centennial Exhibition, had written his own book in awe of the company. He conjured a new romantic vision: 'vast plantations of nodding banana plants'. And this was no mirage. It was the norm in Central America, he noted in his *Conquest of the Tropics: The Story of the Creative Enterprises Conducted by the United Fruit Company*. The 'banana of commerce' represented man's 'profound triumph over nature'. If it weren't for United Fruit the banana would never have emerged from the dark, then arrived in such quantities as to bring prices that made it available to all. To be able to intervene like this in the market system already displayed a supernatural power, since the laws of supply and demand were hitherto thought divine. Now, suggested Adams, they could be both usefully challenged and harnessed.

United Fruit was 'The Machine'. Was it like Corliss's steam engine, perhaps, or like America itself? It 'made no useless motions', Adams wrote, and 'brought together the parts'. Never before had distant pestilential lands been linked with the thriving metropolises of New York and elsewhere in the US. The benighted tropics would be 'civilised' in the process but, crucially, so too would the civilising process come to bear on the US condition. United Fruit had been born not only of the 'Age of Invention', but also of the 'Age of Panics'. These saw the natural order of the market regularly collapse under the weight of 'petty, planless and wasteful competition'. But United Fruit had a plan. It was the 'efficient monopoly' that would craft order from chaos. Its destiny, it appeared, was little less than to save capitalism.

Thus, United Fruit had immediately set about eliminating its rivals. In New Orleans these had preyed on the unfortunate Keith. Now United Fruit came after them. It took over shipping companies and importers and put others out of business. Some formed an anti-United Fruit 'resistance front' to limited avail. Rival ships docked to find United Fruit dropping its prices below anything capable of profit, so forcing them to sell at a loss. When they had sold their cargo, United Fruit would raise its prices. It could afford to destroy fruit to keep prices up, or give it away to stop others selling theirs. By such means the company raised its share of the banana market to between 80 and 90 per cent; effectively all of it.

Many Jamaican growers in Costa Rica had to sell up to Keith. If they didn't like the prices he offered for their bananas, or that he charged for use of his railway, they could always exercise their freedom of choice and leave their fruit to rot. In Panama around Almirante Bay and the Chiriquí Lagoon, Keith pushed small growers out of business by undercutting their prices and buying up their land. Meanwhile, cheap parcels of land officially intended for peasant farmers were purchased by United Fruit's local lawyers in the names of family members and friends and sold on to Keith.

United Fruit captured the spirit of the times. Until recently the US, in its foreign affairs, had been inhibited by history. In 1893 a posse of planters, mainly from the US, had overthrown Hawaii's Queen Liliolukani and called on Washington to annexe the islands. President Cleveland refused: this was no way for an anti-colonial power to be acting. In 1898 President William McKinley had no such qualms and went ahead with the annexation. In the space of 113 days that year, McKinley had successfully fought the Spanish–American War, ejecting Spain from Cuba, Puerto Rico and the Philippines. When the Filipinos protested against US rule merely taking over from that of imperial Spain, McKinley resolved to 'uplift, civilise and Christianise them'.

United Fruit engaged in capturing the nation's hearts and minds. Soon after the company's birth, Keith chartered four new ships from the navy that had not been finished in time for the Spanish–American War. They were bigger than the rest of the company's boats and he had them converted to carrying both cargo and fee-paying passengers. Keith knew the allure of the tropics and anticipated their popular appeal. With the

Great White Fleet, United Fruit steamed into the 'American Century'.

Its latest dictator assassinated, the Guatemalan Cabinet had met in emergency session in February 1898 to choose a successor. One person they had neglected to invite was the minister of the interior, General Manuel Estrada Cabrera. Piqued, Estrada Cabrera stormed in with pistol drawn to save them the agony of further deliberation.

Increased coffee production by Brazil had recently brought prices crashing down. The result for Guatemala was a crisis of spiralling debt and rampant inflation. Like Costa Rica, Guatemala had been building its own railway, though using its coffee to pay for it.

The railway was intended to bridge the nation's class and racial divide. The majority of Guatemala's population was Mayan. They lived in such impoverished provinces as Quiché and Quezaltenango in the mountainous north-west of the country, the Indian Highlands. The Mayans comprised many communities, identities and languages, all agreed in their wish to keep themselves to themselves. 'Guatemala' was a theory devised and imposed on them by others. These others in the main were the sizeable 'ladino' – or 'mestizo' – minority of mixed Indian and Spanish blood. The ladinos regarded the Mayans as backward and lacking in ambition. Over all a 'white' elite, oligarchs of Spanish, British and Scandinavian stock, and also a wealthy community of Germans, ruled the land.

From the Pacific coast in the west, the railway system had already reached Guatemala City, the nation's capital located more or less midway between the coasts. As the line had approached from the Atlantic in the east, the coffee money had run out. The railway had stopped at the tiny settlement of El Rancho, sixty miles short of its goal. Estrada Cabrera invited Minor Keith to finish the job.

It would prove a fateful step for the country but railways were the technology of the day and Keith's terms were matchless. Rather than cash upfront, he asked for merely as much land as it would take to grow his bananas. The plan had a familiar ring. As in Costa Rica, bananas would pay for the railway. Other foreign contractors were only skilled in the ways of railroads and could not offer this integrated approach. For final payment, Keith would take his profits from running the Atlantic side of the railway for ten years following completion. After that it would come under Guatemalan control, in theory, at least.

The implications were not missed at home: 'Americans win in Guatemala', read the *New York Times* headline. Guatemala was broke and, with such vast amounts of Brazilian coffee in the world, would not recover sufficiently to take over its Atlantic railroad even after ten years. By default this vital infrastructure would end up in the hands of Keith and United Fruit.

The contract allowed three years for the work but the reckoning came sooner. Heavy rains, flooding and labour problems dogged the project. President Estrada Cabrera revived old laws to have workers forcibly drafted. Many came from the Indian Highlands and, more used to the elevated coffee plantations, fell sick or died in the humid eastern lowlands. Others ran away to next-door Belize. Keith recruited Jamaicans, as well as Afro-Caribbean workers from the US, but the works from El Rancho dropped behind schedule. He requested an extension to his contract's three-year deadline.

Estrada Cabrera attempted to assume his role as dictator of national events and force the issue, a tactic more successful in the Cabinet room than in the present circumstances of facing a foreign company. He threatened to take the Atlantic contract away from Keith and imagined he could get in other contractors. Britain, Germany and France had their railway builders who had shown interest but the problem remained: what did they know about bananas?

Keith left matters to his appointed representative in Guatemala, Percival Farquahar. While upgrading Preston's railway in Cuba, Keith had met Farquahar working for another company. He had a persuasive line in negotiation. After he had won the contract to electrify Havana's street railway, Farquahar's detractors had accused him of such tactics as bribery and attempted kidnapping. In Guatemala he resorted to a less dark, if still summary manoeuvre that Keith himself had stumbled across by chance in Costa Rica. It would become a regular part of many a multi-national company's armoury. Companies always had the option of departing from whatever country they found themselves in and Farquahar now simply threatened that Keith and United Fruit would pull out of Guatemala.

He had his bags packed and ready to leave in the lobby of his hotel in the centre of Guatemala City at breakfast one morning. Estrada Cabrera's spies, notoriously everywhere, relayed word back to the palace just around the corner. An appointment with the president was arranged for noon.

In the contract signed in 1904, United Fruit named its terms. Keith took full control of the railway on the Atlantic side of the country. This included all rolling stock, stations and telegraph lines, plus the lately constructed Atlantic port of Puerto Barrios. All had been built at national expense. The company gained huge new banana lands. It would pay no taxes to speak of. The government would not have known how to assess them anyway. It waived all rights to view the company's books.

Before long, the company would take over the nation's railroad on the Pacific side, too. The present owners would be happy to sell up, since they had little custom from Guatemala's hard-hit coffee growers, who were mostly located in that region of the country. In future, any growers – of coffee or other products in the west of Guatemala, or of bananas in the east nearer the Atlantic coast – would have to use Keith's railway at prices dictated by United Fruit. The company had effectively assumed control of the means by which much of the country's economic life was conducted.

Shortly after the agreement, Farquahar was called in to explain it over beer and dinner to the oligarchs gathered at the German legation. One by one as the drink flowed they rose to condemn their president's failure to defend the national interest. When Farquahar soberly asserted that no bribes had been involved, he was greeted with gales of laughter. (Estrada Cabrera, sensibly not present at the German legation dinner, later thanked Farquahar for defending his good name.)

The mirthful Germans had had their moment but ultimately knew the laugh was on them. For the sake of plugging the sixty-mile El Rancho gap they and other members of Guatemala's erstwhile ruling elite had lost much of their power. As for the deal, bribes on the whole had been unnecessary. A relatively small inducement to the president was eventually uncovered, but it amounted to a few railway shares, of little more value than a drink. In the judgement of its dictator, Guatemala needed its railway and United Fruit alone had the resources to provide it. Thereafter for the better part of two decades Estrada Cabrera and the company enjoyed a happy coincidence of views on how the country should be run.

Fifty years after the agreement, Miguel Ángel Asturias's book *The Green Pope* featured a contract engineered by a fictitious US railwayman. Asturias named him George Maker Thompson, for which presumably read Minor Cooper Keith. With his Guatemalan escapade, Keith rose yet again in status: from railway builder carving plantations through the tropical forest to 'Green Pope' and maker of governments.

5
The Banana Man

If Minor Keith and Andrew Preston founded the empire of United Fruit in the early twentieth century, then the company's fate and development for much of the next fifty years were in the hands of Sam Zemurray.

Born Samuel Zmurri in 1878 he was brought up in Bessarabia, a region on the Black Sea annexed to Russia. Today parts of it are in Moldova and Romania. In 1903 in his home city of Kishinev, Russia staged one of its worst pogroms and occasioned the first revolt by Russian Jews to defend their community. With an aunt, eleven years earlier, Sam had arrived as a fourteen-year old in New York, where an official of the US immigration department misheard, misspelled and sent him off with a new family name.

He and his aunt headed south to Selma, Alabama, where according to some accounts his uncle had a general store. For a while Zemurray went to work in the Gulf Coast port of Mobile, 130 miles away, swabbing decks on banana boats. Later, with a small fortune of 150 dollars, mainly his uncle's money, he bought enough bananas to fill a railway car but misjudged their ripeness. They were at risk of rotting in the heat before he could get them back to Selma. For a few bunches, he persuaded the train guard to use the telegraph, still a novel invention, to beckon traders out to the stations along the line. He arrived home with no bananas but a thirty-five dollar profit.

'Ripes' and risk were Zemurray's forte. By 1895 at the age of seventeen he was competing on the New Orleans waterfront: 'Fifty stems, I'll take fifty!' He had a thick accent, Russian, some said Romanian. He was mainly conspicuous because of his height of one metre ninety, over six feet. He took the bananas big companies didn't want, those which were too ripe – sold to him cheaply and sometimes even given to him. He was mad, the Banana Man. He bought and sold quickly and soon began to bite into the big companies' profits.

He was comfortable in the south US. Anti-Semitism was the norm but colour prejudice significantly worse. Italians, prominent in the banana business, were also subjected to prejudice. Fears that the fruit brought disease whipped up anti-Italian feeling. As far away to the north as Illinois, banana trains and their Italian crews were stopped from passing through the state during one outbreak of yellow fever.

Soon Zemurray had paid for his mother, grandparents and six brothers and sisters to come to the US. He was the archetypal migrant made good: the individual of humble origin who did it 'on his own'. But he was also smart enough to have befriended Minor Keith. Zemurray's risky investments often left him short of cash and, soon after United Fruit's formation in 1899, he proposed that that it buy a 60 per cent stake in his company, a controlling interest.

Zemurray had his sights on Honduras, which United Fruit was keen to enter. The company monopolised the shipping of fruit from the Honduran Bay Islands and much of that from the mainland, but wanted to grow its own. Honduras's banana production was higher than elsewhere in Central America and was mainly run by local and Italian smallholders operating in a hundred-mile stretch of its northern coast known as Atlántida. The area boomed, especially around the coastal redoubt of Puerto Cortés. On its sickle-shaped promontory, the port attracted some particular types of enterprising people: US engineers who had worked over the years on Honduras's various stop-start schemes to build a national railroad; prostitutes on a downward career path from Marseilles to Port Said; an assortment of ne'er-do-wells who had turned up from the US fleeing the law.

As assessed by United Fruit, the Honduran banana industry was ripe for rationalisation. Producers floated their bananas out on 'lighters', barges, propelled by men with poles to the big boats moored off the Ulúa Bar. The fruit was several days off the plant and headwinds across the Gulf of Mexico might yet ruin it. With investment, small settlements like Tela and Trujillo could be developed into fully-fledged ports of call for banana boats.

Zemurray, the Banana Man, went beyond the coastal fringe into the interior. He learned fluent Spanish. He gave good prices to the producers, and didn't quibble over quality quite like the big guys did. The latter habitually turned lighters back from their boats with a weight of rejected cargo. Zemurray bought and shipped out quickly. He had started with a tramp steamer, moving on with United Fruit's backing to two freighters that were once among the fastest on the Liverpool–Buenos Aires run. Soon he was itching to buy his own plantations.

Sam Zemurray, it was said, was so intent on getting on with the job at hand that he had no eye on posterity. Not much of his early life is known and he left no private papers. Possibly Arthur Miller, the playwright, was speaking for him in *Death of a Salesman* through the ghostly voice of Willy

Loman's brother Ben, the one who made it: 'I went into the jungle at seventeen, and at twenty-one, by God, I came out rich.'

United Fruit suffered its first big blow in 1903, when Panama disease hit its plantations in the country of the same name. Disease was not exactly new, but the big plantations were. On small plots and lots or on scattered plants in the jungle, disease would die out for lack of anywhere to go. United Fruit's huge plantations extended a graphic invitation to disaster – soon Panama disease jumped borders to Costa Rica and headed north to Nicaragua, and beyond.

The same year also saw constructive developments in Panama, from the United Fruit and US point of view. Panamanian insurrectionists backed by the US declared independence from Colombia. Colombia was looking the other way, engaged in its 'Thousand Days War' as centralists and federalists battled to decide which way to run their country. Panama went its own way, or so it seemed.

President Theodore Roosevelt was in the White House. In 1898, the former governor of New York had taken time off from domestic duties to play a US hero's role in the Spanish–American War. In Cuba he had led troops, the 'Rough Riders', in the victorious storming of San Juan Hill. He had returned to be President McKinley's running mate in the election of 1900 and assumed leadership when McKinley was assassinated the following year. The deceased president had put the US on an imperial course and Teddy Roosevelt resolved to continue the adventure.

He had been urging the Colombians to get works going again on a canal across Panama. It would provide the key route for swift passage by ships of the US Navy between the Pacific and Atlantic Oceans. The Colombians baulked at the idea of the waterway on grounds of its potential for increasing US intervention in the region.

Roosevelt intervened anyway. The Panamanian 'insurrection' in late 1903 had been flagged by an announcement in the US press some six months before. At the time of the uprising, the US Navy was primed to keep troops from Colombia at bay. United Fruit's fleet even ran in supplies for the insurrectionists. When the minimal combat had ceased, Panama became a rare recorded instance of a country that declared its independence and gave it up at the same time.

As things stood, a canal across Panama wouldn't have yet been that important to United Fruit. Its plantations were in the distant north-east of the country, well away from the canal's prospective path. For the company it was easier to reach its Panamanian plantations by ship from Boston, than by the rough overland route from Panama City near where the canal would be. Eventually the canal would provide useful access to California but that was still a relatively under-developed market for the company.

The canal scheme soon developed into an unholy row between Roosevelt and United Fruit. The president had wanted to follow Keith's example of hiring Jamaican labour on grounds that there was none better for working in pestilential tropical conditions. Keith, however, needed Jamaicans for his railway in Guatemala and lobbied the British in Jamaica to stop them going to such a 'terrible place' as Panama. Roosevelt was enraged at this treachery.

From Washington, United Fruit had been out of sight and mind but now had inadvertently thrust itself into view. It had strayed from the course of normal business into the realm of 'strategic interests'.

How Roosevelt dealt with United Fruit would be tricky. He couldn't easily argue that the company had stood in the way of the US achieving its imperial destiny, because the very idea was again under scrutiny. His Panama escapade had drawn a lot of critical press, with cartoons of him, the rotund 'Rough Rider' bearing down on poor little Colombia. He had blustered on, saying the US had no choice in its actions – which were 'determined for us by fate'. Joseph Conrad subsequently published his novel *Nostromo* in 1904 with a US financier as one of his characters echoing the sentiment: 'we shall run the world's business whether the world likes it or not . . . the world can't help it – and neither can we, I guess.'

But the president had another stick with which to strike at the company. In his days as New York governor, Roosevelt was the reputed 'trust buster'. He had warmly embraced the new anti-trust legislation of the 1890s and attacked big companies for monopolistic practices. Now was a good time for a repeat performance. Keen to make an example of United Fruit, Roosevelt put his anti-trust investigators on the case.

With Keith usually in tropical absentia, Andrew Preston assumed responsibility for guarding the company's US flank. He tempered the US government's belligerence by taking evasive action. In recent years United Fruit had bought control of several companies, like Sam Zemurray's, while leaving day-to-day management in their hands. Preston now proceeded to sell control of some of them back to the original owners. One, Italian-run and mainly operating in Honduras, ambitiously named itself the Standard Fruit

Company, while remaining too small to be a rival. Another company was Zemurray's but he hadn't the cash to pay for United Fruit's share. So, he remained in the company's debt and in secret partnership.

1907 saw a further setback to the Honduran ambitions of both Sam Zemurray and United Fruit. The president and dictator, General Manuel Bonilla, was overthrown. He had been a friend of the thriving community of foreign entrepreneurs on the Honduran Atlantic coast and had a particular rapport with Zemurray. Minor Keith was another pioneer of coastal enterprise, with his trading post in Bluefields, Nicaragua, and others in Guatemala, Costa Rica and Panama.

The word was that President Bonilla had been well rewarded for his patronage of such commercial talents. Critics churlishly called this bribery. Others countered that it was merely tribute, in due acknowledgement of the leader's power and position. A rebellion from within the Honduran armed forces took the distinctly anti-Bonilla line and, backed by an invasion from the south by Nicaragua's army, forced the president to flee in 1907. A US gunboat spirited him away from the country and soon he turned up in New Orleans. Here he became a familiar face, in early old age and with greying hair and moustache, around the bars and other funhouses of the city's Vieux Carré.

Both Honduras and Nicaragua had had differences of opinion with the foreign business people on their Atlantic seaboards. At times these expatriates seemed to want to run things as if the coastal region were an independent state.

It was debatable whether Honduras had been well served on its Atlantic side by 'gringo' enterprise. In the case of its railway, for example, the region had a few dozen miles of line but these followed the meandering course of local rivers. John C. Trautwine, a US railroad builder, constructed many of them. The Hondurans had commissioned him to build a line inland to Tegucigalpa but made the mistake of paying him by the mile. His line wound around the coastal flatlands studiously avoiding the escarpment that led to the capital. When the contract money ran out, Trautwine retired home, a rich man. He even wrote a best-selling manual on the art of building the 'permanent way'.*

Such tricks left Tegucigalpa stranded on its high plateau. Protected behind its three peaks and basking on moonlit nights in the echo of gentle church bells, it was a pleasant city, although difficult to regard as a capital.

In the conduct of its foreign business, United Fruit was soon again in radical mode. It stepped up a gear in Europe. In 1903 it had bought a half share in the British company Fyffes, whose Jamaican plantations had been badly damaged by hurricanes. Fyffes supplied the British market and also had plantations in the Canary Islands. United Fruit took full control of the company in 1910.

At the same time, the Caribbean islands were proving problematic. They were full of smallholders who got in the way and produced inefficiently by United Fruit's standards. They were apt to complain to their governments about the company's overbearing presence. In Cuba the company stopped growing bananas and planted sugar cane instead. United Fruit's banana production was migrating west towards

* If many read it, few copied him. Most of the world's railways are built on either a standard or narrow gauge. Trautwine had his own, known as 'bastard gauge'.

the wider open spaces of Central America, and would continue to do so.

United Fruit went on the warpath in Panama. This was near the disputed border with Costa Rica. It would have been easier just to see the area as United Fruit territory, yet, rashly, a US rival had chosen not to do so. The provocatively named American Banana Company, ABC, attempted to set up in Panama by the frontier with Costa Rica and near United Fruit's plantations. Having competently cleared jungle and laid railway line, ABC simply hadn't done its homework about the general lie of the land. Costa Rican troops appeared one day, ejected ABC and handed its assets to United Fruit.

ABC sought legal redress in the US. Its chances looked good. In 1909 Teddy Roosevelt had been succeeded by the administration of President William Taft, who was prepared to get tough on big company bullying. Standard Oil would be broken up in 1911. But United Fruit? Taft was a lawyer from provincial Ohio. He said he had never wanted the job of president and pined for the day when he could leave it and go home. He had no general interest in foreign affairs, let alone the particularities of Central America. Against such an executive backdrop ABC took United Fruit all the way to the Supreme Court. The case was thrown out, with such distant squabbles considered 'beyond jurisdiction'.

United Fruit sensed it was time to get back on the offensive in Honduras. Panama disease had spread further across Central America and just reached Guatemala. Honduras was the only major producer left free of the plague.

Minor Keith sallied forth with what was fast becoming his party piece: a railroad-for-land scheme. Honduras would get its railway to Tegucigalpa and virtually anywhere it wanted;

Keith would get large swathes of the country. By now, however, the Hondurans had the working examples of Costa Rica and Guatemala to go by and turned him down.

In 1910, therefore, United Fruit adopted a different approach. Sam Zemurray suddenly arrived in Honduras. To some extent he was on a mission of his own. He was determined to go back into the jungle and enrich himself further by producing his own bananas. But he was heavily indebted to United Fruit, with whom he had been in clandestine alliance since United Fruit had sold his company back to him in return for an IOU.

Zemurray had two hundred thousand dollars to invest, some of which had been raised from banks in Mobile, New Orleans and New York. The rest came from 'secondary financiers', loan sharks charging interest rates of fifty per cent. He bought expanses of virgin land and went to Tegucigalpa to claim the usual tax concessions. Without them, the jungle clearance work, the drainage and irrigation, the building of railways and workers' huts and all the other paraphernalia of banana production would have been simply impossible.

For some reason, difficult to understand from the perspective of the Banana Man and United Fruit, the Hondurans turned him down. Zemurray was especially perplexed; he faced financial ruin.

O. Henry was first to use the term 'banana republic', in his only novel, *Cabbages and Kings* (1904). The popular and prolific US short-story writer referred to the 'maritime banana republic' of Anchuria, which was his imaginary version of Honduras. He portrayed it as a place of friendly natives and loveable rogues, the latter mainly from the United States.

O. Henry had lived in Puerto Cortés and met these adventurers. He was on the run from the law himself, and later returned to the US to face a charge of stealing funds from the bank in Texas where he had worked as a clerk. He served a three-year jail sentence, though subsequent suggestions were that his offence was more a bookkeeping error than a crime. When he wrote *Cabbages and Kings*, and was being charitable about its characters, he was seeking similar redemption for himself.

O. Henry wrote at the end of his book of a coup d'état in Anchuria orchestrated by the 'Vesuvius Fruit Company'. He described the company in mildly critical but overall understanding tones: 'the power that forever stood with chiding smile and uplifted finger to keep Anchuria in the class of good children'. And its coup was for the best of reasons: by the gift of the company a tyrant was removed, the right man found to replace him and everyone's best interests served.

The tale played well to his readership. If US public opinion developed a contemporary view on United Fruit's role and that of the US itself in Central America, O. Henry played his part in framing it.

In Cortés he came across the likes of Lee Christmas, son of a Louisiana cotton planter from near Baton Rouge. Christmas had come to Honduras to drive trains on John C. Trautwine's railway but was colour-blind and at some disadvantage in a vocation dependent on signals and flags. He went into mercenary matters, had a knack for it and enjoyed uncommon luck. In one rebellion Christmas had been captured and put before a firing squad. 'Don't bury my body!' he responded to the request for his final wish: 'so the buzzards can shit me on your heads', or words to similar effect. His captors were impressed, possibly unnerved, and let him go.

Christmas had worked for ex-President Bonilla, now banished. He had been made a general, rode a white horse on ceremonial days and a dark blue uniform tailored in Paris. He had been Bonilla's head of security in Tegucigalpa. Christmas had once foiled a plot against Bonilla, so it was written, when he stormed the congress, arrested several deputies and threw them in jail. But he was more at home in the sweaty climes of the coast. The company he kept included Guy 'Machine-gun' Molony of New Orleans. Molony had gone to fight with the British in South Africa during the Boer Wars at the turn of the century. Twice injured, once nearly fatally, he had returned to be nearer home and hawk his passion for rapid fire around the revolutions of Central America. Both Christmas and Molony relished such fights. It was just a question of finding someone to finance them.

When, in 1910, Sam Zemurray materialised in Honduras with his two hundred thousand dollars and his plan for jungle development, it turned out that it was not the Hondurans who rejected his request for tax concessions at all. Honduras was only playing to a script written by Washington, and what happened next amounted to the United Fruit Company and Zemurray making war on their own government.

Such revolutions as had deposed ex-President Bonilla in 1907, and such ruses as had left railwayman Trautwine a rich man, had also left Honduras deeply in debt, not least to bankers in Europe. Washington feared that those bankers' countries might just be inspired militarily to intervene on their behalf and collect the money.

To deter such a threat, the US government had a plan, part of its present policy of 'Dollar Diplomacy'. Some reputable agency, appointed by Washington, would occupy Honduras's custom houses and, with the full agreement of the home country, maximise and collect its tax revenues. For an agreed and generous fee, this agency would make sure that foreign bankers and other creditors were paid and, therefore, eliminate the need for aggressive intervention. The scheme was in the hands of President Taft's foreign affairs specialist, Philander Knox, the secretary of state, and it was called the 'Knox Plan'.

The reputable (if not universally regarded as such) agency appointed to set up shop in the Honduran counting houses was J. P. Morgan, the bankers. When Zemurray requested tax concessions, therefore, it was J. P. Morgan that turned him down. It was a bank and it was in Honduras for the serious purpose of organising the nation's finances, not listening to fanciful schemes of plantations rising from the jungle.

Zemurray reacted furiously. A lone entrepreneur, he argued, he faced bankruptcy at the hands of a 'nasty trust'. He was the spirit of American enterprise, not some 'favourite son of J. P. Morgan', he raged: 'I've never even met Mr Morgan.' He sent lobbyists to meet whoever they could while loitering in the halls of Congress. He came to Washington himself, and took his plea directly to secretary of state Knox. No record suggests he ever met Knox. According to Zemurray, their encounter led to a meeting of minds. Knox, he said, even gave the nod to his next course of action, which was hardly likely since it entailed rudely abandoning the Knox Plan. The Banana Man planned to buy a boat, fill it with assorted mercenaries and crooks and overthrow the US-supported Honduran government itself.

Bonilla waited in exile in New Orleans. With him were Christmas and Molony, minus his machine-gun, since they were under observation by the US secret service. Zemurray purchased a large motorised yacht called the *Hornet*, built in the 1890s for one of the railway robber barons. It had also seen service for the US Navy in the Spanish-American War. On an uncommonly cold winter's night around the New Year of 1911, Bonilla and friends waved the *Hornet* off from the quay. The boat's master had lodged an official sailing plan for a small excursion eastwards along the Gulf Coast.

Bonilla, Christmas and Molony repaired to Madame May Evans's lodgings of entertainment on Basin Street in the old quarter. The secret service agent tailing them watched shivering from across the street till the early hours. When he phoned his office – 'It's nothing but a drunken party' – he was told to go home. Within minutes, Bonilla's party had left Madame May's to take a fast launch also provided by Zemurray. They outpaced a watching vessel of the coastguard and caught up with the *Hornet* off Biloxi, Mississippi.

The three friends landed near Roatán in the Honduran Bay Islands. They joined rebel forces to begin an assault on the nearby port of Trujillo. William Walker, 'King of Nicaragua', had been put against its castle wall and shot in the 1860s. A question hung over whether this mission would enjoy better luck. A gunboat, the USS *Tacoma*, seized the *Hornet*. Bonilla and comrades, however, were allowed to go on their way. The *Tacoma*'s lingering offshore presence proved a better deterrent to the Honduran defence forces, many members of which did not emerge from their coastal forts.

United Fruit landed a company of men and guns raised by Minor Keith from company plantations in Guatemala. Puerto Cortés, meanwhile, was alert to the appearance of adopted sons Christmas and Molony from across the eastern horizon. In sporadic fighting one US resident was killed. Talks to 'separate the sides', or rather, to arrange for the government's step-down, were held aboard the USS *Tacoma*. Thus a force of 'patriots' marched off triumphant on the ascending road to Tegucigalpa.

His plan scuppered, Knox promised a 'full investigation'. At the same time, President Taft had no desire to get involved in such far-flung events. Washington adopted the course of least resistance. What was the point in doing otherwise? All that was happening was that control of a small and largely unknown country's affairs was passing from the hands of a large US banking house to an aspirant bunch of Banana Men. At first blush, it even appeared that the cause against oppressive big business was being served.

The Honduran coup successfully carried out, Zemurray had no trouble getting his tax concessions and go-ahead to develop his lands. Elections were staged to confirm Bonilla as president and he granted Zemurray whatever he wanted. The Banana Man was put in charge of national finances, his first job being to raise the government loan that would pay his expenses incurred in the invasion.

Perhaps the keenest protests against the coup came from an unlikely quarter. The US entrepreneurs of the Atlantic Coast had initially supported the exercise. It had seemed perfectly fine to them that a force with interests like theirs was keeping Honduras 'in the class of good children'. Until they realised just who that force was. Behind Sam Zemurray loomed the might of United Fruit.

The company denied all involvement in events. Yet, for a party that had nothing to do with anything, United Fruit was handsomely rewarded. Zemurray presented the company with two large concessions of land, at Tela and Trujillo. With them the Banana Man cleared his debts – and United Fruit was soon hacking its way into the Honduran interior.

The Honduran invasion marked an important development in United Fruit's world. Costa Rica and Guatemala had previously succumbed to banana republicanism through a mix of happenstance, ill fortune and stealth. Panama had had its 'insurrection', but conspiracy and violence were more the means by which Honduras had been pulled into the company fold. For good measure, US marines, briefly sent to Honduras to 'keep the peace', were soon landing south along Central America's Atlantic coast in Nicaragua, a country deemed to have been causing too much trouble in the region. The marines were to stay in Nicaragua for over twenty years.

The events of 1911 in Honduras brought to an end what might be termed the United Fruit Company's 'nice guy' period. There would be little more of that. United Fruit had established its power and was of every mind to wield it.

6
Taming the Enclave

United Fruit much preferred to do things its way, which on its distant enclaves was generally possible. Inefficient and bungling, the state lacked the company's understanding and touch, and any interference was ignored.

One sphere in which United Fruit excelled was in the handling of labour. It had its own labour laws and any that its host countries might have had were suspended in United Fruit's areas. It hired, fired and controlled through its own security forces, a network of charge-hands, superintendents, police and spies. The latter were known as *oidos en el suelo*, 'ears in the ground', whose function was not only to be listening out for political troublemakers, but also those who complained too much about working conditions.

United Fruit had recruited far and wide in its effort to discover the most cost-effective and productive workforce. Minor Keith's first experiments with ill-fated recruits from the sleazier side of New Orleans had succeeded in little more than reducing the size of the US criminal fraternity.

In Costa Rica, General Guardia had urged him to import reliable Europeans, especially Swiss, Germans and British. Instead Keith had pursued the cheaper option of getting Costa Rica to overturn laws forbidding Asian immigration. Itinerant Chinese had built the US's transcontinental railroad but had raised fears that suddenly hordes of them would flood into

Central America and the Caribbean. The Chinese were duly allowed into Costa Rica, to become the worst treated of all workers on the railroad. Regarded as racially inferior, they suffered the more for being far from home and from anywhere where they could lodge a complaint. 'I present to you in irons the following Chinese,' wrote a works superintendent to Keith of one group who had committed some unspecified offence, 'whip them as you see fit.'

The Italians Keith hired from Piedmont were thought to be of a higher breed. His application to the Costa Rican government to allow them in commended them for being 'from a cold climate': they were in the habit of working hard to keep warm. They would also be 'bettering the racial stock' of Costa Rica by mixing 'with the rest of the natives'. He drew a comparison with the government recently importing pedigree cattle to improve local herds.

Race became a key issue. In Guatemala, Highland Indians were 'weak'. At home they might walk miles each day up and down their volcanoes carrying firewood and water, but they couldn't adapt to conditions on the plains. Ladinos didn't arrive looking for work on the banana plantations till the jungle had been cleared and the hospital built. Held to be among the most useless were Afro-Americans, 'uppity' and spoiled by their association with US life. Other black labour was indirectly tainted. Caribbeans who had worked on the Panama Canal under US management had been 'pampered' by the experience.

Thus the British West Indian surged to the top of the most popular worker list, not only because of his physical resilience. He was said to be 'extremely courteous'. This was attributed to a 'triumph of empire', its assumed old decencies and manners, and also to Keith's 'charisma'. Keith took on a guise akin to that of an imperial viceroy. With his plans to build a railway the length of the region, he acquired a new nomenclature: the 'Cecil Rhodes of Central America'.

The reality behind the legend was that the Jamaicans caused trouble and they complained about conditions, sometimes to the British back in Jamaica and occasionally to passing ships of the Royal Navy. They could always take a steamer home, or move on to different work in, say, Panama. But work at home was not plentiful or well paid. If they could find employment on the Caribbean islands, amid the sugar gluts and other economic crises, they were likely to be paid twenty cents a day.

United Fruit paid such wages for one to two hours' work. Yet the company did not lose. Following the Civil War, United Fruit served the function of 'exporting' and, as it were, 'rebranding' slavery. The old system had become regarded as both brutal and inefficient. It was expensive to have a workforce around whether there was work to be done or not and expecting bed and board. In the new era, United Fruit provided basic bunkhouse facilities, hired and fired at will and had its workers spend their wages at the company store. United Fruit paid in 'scrip', pieces of paper for exchange at the store where the company named its prices. The stores made good profit. Their standards varied, some being just rough counters where workers bought basic items. Others were department stores, with silk shirts and ties on the counters, tropical suits and felt hats displayed on dummies and, in some, comfy chairs peculiarly ranged on upper shelves. Prices for such items were out of reach for all except the white managerial few.

Members of the upper echelons of management were generally the products of the US's better schools. Young men of the right type were sent down to sweat it out in the tropics, rather as their British counterparts were despatched to Aden and other points 'east of Suez' as an exercise in character formation. The most junior rose at five to harness their mules by moonlight and head off for a day's arguing with the cutters and carriers over the quality and quantity of stems harvested. The prospect was that they might make it to the top and, within ten years, control of a whole country could be theirs. Or they might fall by the wayside and seek wisdom from the bottoms of glasses in the bars of Puerto Cortés.

As for the company's lower-level managers, who had direct control over the workforce, United Fruit held a particular fascination for whites from the US South. It recruited liberally from among them. Such overseers were either of an age to remember the days of slavery, or had been brought up in its aftermath. Many were of a mentality to regret its passing.

Jungle clearance work was the hardest and most likely to cause discontent among the workforce. The risks from snakes were at their highest. At two and half metres long, the *barba amarilla*, or fer-de-lance, was easily recognisable with its yellow throat markings, but would you see it? Venomously allied to the rattlesnake, it had no rattle to announce its presence. About one in four workers received treatment for malaria. While clearing land, they lived in hastily constructed palm-thatched huts that gave minimal protection against the swarms of mosquitoes. As market demand for bananas rose rapidly, new lands were constantly being cleared.

Work in the ports depended on the arrival and departure of ships. The call of the siren summoned stevedores to the docks at any hour of the day or night. Jobs were handed out on the basis of first come, first hired. On the plantations, cutting and carrying gangs began work at short notice and worked till the required shipload of stems had been cut, carried and transported to the docks in railroad cars.

Stories of discontent could, like scrip, be swapped at the company store. These were sensitive places. Disturbances broke out in 1910 on United Fruit plantations in Guatemala after six hundred Jamaicans gathered to complain about prices and looted two stores. Against its first instincts, the company called for the local military commander to make arrests. He said he wouldn't do so for fear of setting off further violence. The company settled things, therefore, in its own manner. A group of ladinos seized William Wright, a Jamaican worker, and lynched him. The police arrested one of those involved and released him a few days later. United Fruit hired the man as a farm superintendent.

Such events remained hidden from the people at home, where United Fruit had managed to create a quite different impression. In 1912 the company had cleared the jungle to reveal the Mayan ruins of Quiriguá in eastern Guatemala. Magnificent stone monoliths spoke of an ancient civilisation built by 'master races' from afar, said *National Geographic* magazine. Other comment drew comparison between the 'mighty race of people' that centuries ago had built Quiriguá and the 'new civilisation' forged by United Fruit.

Early in its own life, the company had discovered the virtue of selfless acts of philanthropy. It had saved a precious remnant of a nation's heritage. But grand gestures in the cause of culture aside, it was also keen to identify with that of the common man.

In the US, concern for the treatment of workers was rising. Work conditions and hours, the attitude of employers, especially large companies towards their employees, and opportunities for social and educational improvement were exercising the public mind. Cooper Union, a university in New York City for students of humble background – Edison had studied there – had provided the platform for the first workers' rights campaigns. In Cooper Union's Great Hall the great and the good addressed the concerns of ordinary people. Presidents Lincoln and Roosevelt had spoken there during their election campaigns. President Woodrow Wilson had just taken office at the start of 1913 and would soon be the first incumbent to speak at Cooper Union. But in July an organisation called the Banana Buyers Protective Association beat him to it and argued the case for the labouring poor.

Ironically, a rally four years before in 1909 at Cooper Union had seen the birth of the National Association for the Advancement of Coloured Peoples. One of the NAACP's main campaigns was to abolish the practice of lynching in the US South. It was less than a year later that William Wright was lynched in Guatemala, apparently with the approval of United Fruit.

In the guise of the Banana Buyers Protective Association, United Fruit took the offensive now against a more elevated enemy. President Wilson had had the audacity to put a tax on bananas. He regarded the fruit as a 'luxury' and aimed to use the monies for reforms to improve conditions for the poor. His plan backfired. Speakers from organisations representing the welfare of children and the struggle of housewives to make ends meet rose to condemn a penalty against the people Wilson claimed to protect. Almost everyone ate bananas. At the turn of the century, the US had imported eighteen million stems a year but by 1913 the figure was forty-two million. This amounted to four billion 'golden satisfiers of American desire', proclaimed the president of the Banana Buyers Protective Association. 'Smite us not with a tariff on bananas.'

Few at the time missed the historical resonance. Seventeen years earlier William Jennings Bryan, the populist politician, had made his famous speech on behalf of the labouring masses and in repudiation of the Gold Standard: 'you shall not crucify mankind upon a cross of gold'. Bryan, now nearing the end of his political career, was Wilson's secretary of state.

Bryan soon found himself deluged with delegations of concerned leaders from the states of Central America and the Caribbean. The tax meant ruin for their countries, they insisted. Influential US advocates of good relations between the Americas, north and south, took the case to the Congress in Washington. Prior to banana cultivation, they explained, the countries to the south had been lands of 'shiftless peoples' and 'haunts of incipient revolutions'. This seemed to imply that United Fruit had changed all that. The exploits of the likes of Lee Christmas and Sam 'the Banana Man' Zemurray went unmentioned.

President Wilson had misread the company's power. He calculated that the public mood was in line with that of presidential 'trust busters' Roosevelt and Taft before him and that he could not fail to win sympathy by taking on another 'nasty trust'. To his surprise he discovered that United Fruit's lobbyists had convinced enough people that the company was actually a benevolent one.

The *New York Times* opined that if the 'trust' in question, United Fruit, did trade in luxuries, then it was for the poor, who were 'entitled to their little luxuries'. The president capitulated. 'JOY MESSAGE FROM WASHINGTON', beamed the headline in the *New York Sun*. 'THE TAX IS OFF!'

By chance, violent strikes simultaneously hit United Fruit in its former lands of 'shiftless peoples' and 'incipient revolutions', and its response was less than benevolent. On the other hand, United Fruit was certainly acting by now like a true multi-national. To address one crisis in Panama, it brought in strike-breakers from Nicaragua and called for troops from Costa Rica. To counter a strike in Costa Rica, it shipped in workers from the distant island of St Kitts. On their long journey across the width of the Caribbean, they did not know what they were sailing into. They refused to disembark when United Fruit's courteous Jamaicans stoned their boat.

In Guatemala, meanwhile, United Fruit workers went on strike after the company decided they were going soft; possibly it had pampered them through association with US life. Guatemalan stevedores were paid by means of a rate per day. It was one dollar twenty five cents for ten hours carrying stems from the railway cars to the ships. The company concluded that the 'day-rate' system was wrong for all concerned. United Fruit was not getting the effort from its workers that it deserved as creator of their employment opportunities, and the workers surely craved the incentive of 'piece rates' to prosper. The company fixed rates at twenty-five cents for each one hundred stems carried. Corporate experts on time and motion had calculated that each man could carry seven hundred stems a day. A worker would pocket one dollar seventy-five cents, a clear half a dollar profit over what he would have made on day rate. In practice no workers could carry a daily seven hundred stems, some managing only two hundred.

When the workers stopped work in protest, United Fruit appealed for help from the local military. Again the commander of the area refused to respond, so the company went directly to its friend, the dictator Manuel Estrada Cabrera. This was contrary to United Fruit's better judgement as a body that didn't put much faith in the power of the state. But the general had reached this stage in his career by showing he was a man of purpose. He had by now wiped out all effective opposition to his regime. He had had one former liberal president hunted down and knifed to death in Mexico City. A chief US diplomat had gone home when it was learned he was being gradually poisoned – on the dictator's say-so. Now that it came to strike-breaking, however, Estrada Cabrera counselled caution. Otherwise things could deteriorate into violence, he suggested. The company's inflamed workforce maybe had a point. United Fruit should return to its day-rate system.

On the plantations the company's white community were aghast. The strikes had alarmed them. They protested to the company that the perpetrators could have killed every one of them and made off without fear of retribution from the national authorities. The message may well have got through. Soon more trouble broke out, this time on a United Fruit plantation when a ladino killed a Jamaican after a card game. A group of Jamaicans set out for revenge and the company called for troops. They arrived in the night, firing indiscriminately into workers' sleeping quarters, wounding and killing an unspecified number. The company now sniffed at this senseless slaughter. It 'amounted to cold-blooded murder', said its chief of Guatemalan operations. It wasn't how United Fruit would have done it.

It was a threatening world and United Fruit's confidence in President Wilson's ability to handle it was limited. From the company's point of view he took an absurdly moralistic stance on international affairs. In such matters, Wilson had his staunch enemies and United Fruit its firm friends in the US Congress. Among them were the likes of Senator Henry Cabot Lodge, of the finest Boston stock and an authority on foreign policy. On the whole, it was Cabot Lodge's opinion that the outside world was best left alone. It was like the old maps had said: 'There Be Demons'.

The Panama Canal finally opened in 1914 but Wilson overrode a plan for US boats to pass through it free of charge. He claimed this was a matter of fairness and US treaty obligations to other powers. But what about the good money that would have to be paid by US ships? United Fruit used the canal more than most.

The president appeared prone to making high-flown statements. He publicly condemned Dollar Diplomacy and called for a more sensitive attitude towards the small nations of Central America and the Caribbean. Things went particularly wrong for United Fruit in Costa Rica after a dictator, General Federico Tinoco, seized power in 1917. He did so with the company's support but not that of President Wilson.

Now into his second term, President Wilson had a new secretary of state, Robert Lansing. When Lansing later returned to private practice, he would act as Minor Keith's legal counsel. For the time being Lansing was intent on advancing the career of his nephew, John Foster Dulles, an up-and-coming lawyer who harboured political ambitions. Dulles enjoyed remarkably good access to President Wilson. He had been down to Costa Rica, ostensibly on an assignment for the New York law firm that employed him, but had also taken time to do some surveillance work: general ears-to-the-ground stuff and quiet engagement of those 'in the know'.

Dulles reported back to his uncle and to the president: these were uncertain times; revolution was at large; across the US's southern border, Mexico's revolution had been going on for seven years; what of the unrest in Russia, the rise of the Bolsheviks, and what might the wider effects be in the US's 'backyard'? Wilson was aware of the issues. Dulles's presentation, fresh from his bit of Central American spying, advocated that Washington should come down firmly on the side of the new Costa Rican dictatorship. Strangely, this argued the line of none other than United Fruit. Reports differ on the extent to which Dulles's uncle Robert agreed or disagreed. Wilson, however, ignored this junior lawyer's counsel. The president imposed a trade ban on Costa Rica and the Tinoco regime fell, succeeded by one with more democratic ideas.

Wilson's critics saw him as a fanatical do-gooder on both domestic and overseas issues. He announced more anti-trust laws and powers to police big business. His programme included an eight-hour working day and cuts in child labour hours. As Wilson carried his idealism abroad, so it became more grandiose. He took the US into the First World War. The US had arrived late, three years into the conflict in 1917, a factor that reflected the large body of domestic opinion that the US should keep out of Old World affairs entirely. No sooner had the war finished in 1918, thanks to the US's decisive intervention, than Wilson was proposing the US maintain the peace, and through nothing less than world government. This was to be his 'League of Nations'.

The First World War had deeply shocked the US. There had, of course, been the distant loss of life but the threat had also reached closer to home. German U-boats had penetrated the psychological wire that the US had put up around itself and the Americas and had attacked shipping. Submarine activity in the Caribbean had, for example, all but killed the banana trade. In July 1918, as the war approached its end, the *Boston Globe* was inspired to headline the arrival of the first United Fruit steamer for a very long while, which was carrying twenty thousand stems from Colombia.

However, it was the intangible elements among the war's legacy to the world that were the most worrying. The Bolshevik revolution had been followed by more violence in Russia and much discontent beyond. The problem with the revolution's dangerous ideas was that you couldn't see them. They blew in on the wind and burrowed up from beneath. They came in the form of 'agitators'.

United Fruit became increasingly paranoid that agitators were everywhere. Like the disease that attacked its plantations, they arose for no reason but to destroy. Strikes in Bocas del Toro in Panama spiralled out of control. The company made arrests, burned the living quarters of workers and rooted up their small plots of land. Several workers died, others fled into the foothills. Unrest spread along the Atlantic coast from Panama to Limón in Costa Rica, with reports of Jamaicans forced to work at the point of a bayonet. The company agreed to mediation by one of the Jamaicans' church ministers, then had him arrested. The Jamaicans appealed to the British, who had set up a consulate in Limón. United Fruit reluctantly agreed to accept the consul as a mediator. His judgement only convinced the company that it should have done things its own way and without this outside intervention. The British consul chided United Fruit. He noted that in the four years since 1914, wages had frozen and prices in the company stores doubled: 'your agitators have most splendid material'.

In 1918 United Fruit's banana workers in Colombia also went on strike – and with a familiar array of demands. They wanted an eight-hour day, the kind of thing President Wilson had been proposing in the US. United Fruit, on the other hand, stood for the view that such nonsense could not be allowed to prevail abroad, in the remote periphery where it was battling to keep capitalism alive. The plantation workers also wanted a six-day week and health provisions. These were the employment terms of white plantation managers; only agitators could have come up with such demands.

United Fruit reckoned to know what it was talking about. After Minor Keith had taken over Colombia's plantations in the late nineteenth century, there were not enough local workers in the Santa Marta region to fill the available jobs. Such small towns as Ciénaga and Aracataca saw their population swell with migrants from other areas of the country and abroad. They weren't universally liked, especially those who would go throwing around their wages to attract local girls, but many drew suspicions for other reasons. Syrians, Lebanese, Italians, Spaniards and others had come from overseas and United Fruit's spies said that especially the Spaniards and Italians had anarchists among them. United Fruit's response to the 1918 strike in Colombia was to stand firm, effectively by doing nothing. After the First World War, markets needed a while to pick up and the company left fruit to rot on the plantations. Its labourers eventually trailed back to work.

In Washington the death-blow was delivered to President Wilson's supreme plan for a League of Nations. Senator Henry Cabot Lodge rose to do the deed in his capacity as chairman of the Senate foreign relations committee. Pillar of the Boston Establishment and from one of its enduring dynasties, Cabot

Lodge viewed the world in the way of his hometown company. Sometimes there was just no dealing with those who would cause trouble, other than to ignore them or remove them from mind. President Wilson had shunned advice to keep out of the First World War and now would have to be firmly dissuaded from his nostrums for peace. Cabot Lodge raised a series of obstacles, the 'Lodge reservations', to the League of Nations idea. At the end of 1919 Wilson had suffered paralysis and had to observe from his sick bed as his big plan failed to win the necessary votes in the Congress.

The US withdrew to police its own bit of the world and, from United Fruit's experience, there was quite enough to be going on with there. US naval patrols had been stepped up along Central America's Atlantic Coast. In 1920, Manuel Estrada Cabrera was thrown out of power in Guatemala, where he had served the company well since he had invited it in twenty years before. As an old friend United Fruit endured some discomfort as rioters ransacked its plantation offices and turned up evidence of company favours to the dictator. Far worse was the disturbing emergence among the activists of apparently Bolshevik ideas. When United Fruit's Guatemalan dock-workers went on strike in the company's Atlantic port of Puerto Barrios, it was not for the usual pay demands or cheaper prices at company stores. They demanded an end to United Fruit's monopoly of Guatemala's railway and ports. This was political; someone, something must be behind it and it called for a concerted response.

Robert Lansing, the former secretary of state was back in private law practice and doing sterling work on Minor Keith's behalf through old contacts at the State Department. Guatemala's revolt simmered and threatened until 1923 when it was ended by resort to old-fashioned gunboat diplomacy. The moment saw the reappearance of the USS *Tacoma*, the man-of-war involved in the Honduran invasion a dozen years before. Docking in Puerto Barrios on a 'routine visit', the *Tacoma*'s captain and a detachment of armed men took Keith's railway to Guatemala City to express goodwill to the military regime. The strike collapsed as its leaders were arrested and shipped south to Bluefields, Nicaragua.

In October 1928 thirty-two thousand United Fruit plantation workers in Santa Marta, Colombia, resuscitated the call for an eight-hour day, a six-day week and free medical treatment which had been unsuccessful ten years earlier. They also went on strike for wages in cash, rather than scrip exchangeable at the company store, and functioning toilets as enjoyed in the homes of plantation overseers. These were boom times for the banana market and economies in general. United Fruit's workers reckoned not to have received their due share of the benefits. The company dismissed their demands as the work of communists and anarchists and had troops occupy the Santa Marta banana zone to maintain order.

In the US, President Calvin Coolidge would soon leave Washington to return to Boston. He had come to the White House on the death of President Warren Harding in 1923 and was about to complete one of its quieter periods of occupancy. He was originally from the Vermont side of the Coolidge family, though had moved to Boston in his early political career and shared the city Brahmins' passion for the understated. A man of very few words, he proudly lived up to the Coolidges' reputation for being 'scions of silence'.

Political speechmaking required Coolidge at times to

depart from form and inevitably opened the way for trouble. History would judge critically his final State of the Union address delivered on December 4, 1928: 'no Congress of the United States has met with a more pleasing prospect than that which appears at the present time,' he had said, adding that at home the US was enjoying a period of tranquillity and contentment. The US had been living through the 'Roaring '20s' and the 'Jazz Age', so 'tranquillity' was stretching the point, but Coolidge's thoughts would be mainly remembered for failing to spot signs of the Wall Street Crash ten months away.

Few noticed how 'in the foreign field', as he called it, Coolidge got it immediately wrong. Here there was peace and 'goodwill that comes from mutual understanding'. He based this claim on the work of Frank Kellogg, his secretary of state. There was actually limited peace and goodwill in the world in the 1920s, with civil war in Russia, the collapse of the postwar German economy and putsches by the extremes of European left and right. The secretary had travelled the globe, however, collecting signatures on his Kellogg Peace Pact. Sixty-nine countries joined this loose coalition of the willing, all agreeing on the need to wage peace.

The resonance of Coolidge's words had hardly faded when messages and telegrams between the US embassy in the Colombian capital Bogotá, its consulate in Santa Marta and the State Department in Washington were relaying details of deepening crisis in the banana zone. Such communications obeyed diplomatic convention: they had 'the honor to report' this, or asked that they might 'respectfully suggest' that. But beneath the polite veneer, there was clearly not a lot of mutual understanding in this area of United Fruit's world.

Additional troops were being drafted into the Santa Marta banana zone to protect US interests. The embassy indicated that it was being kept fully informed of developments by United Fruit. The character of the strike had changed to display a subversive element. Mobs had attacked and burned company stores and management quarters on two United Fruit farms. An engineer, Erasmo Coronel, had been killed. Americans who lived in the area had had to defend themselves for six hours before escaping the banana zone.

The Santa Marta consulate requested a US warship to stand off shore. Colombian sources reported the boat had arrived and some thought they spotted two. Yet Kellogg had refused the request, indicating gunboats were unnecessary because the Colombians were handling matters well enough.

After Sunday mass on the night of December 6 in the small banana town of Ciénaga, strikers, members of their families and other supporters gathered to demonstrate in the main plaza, located near the railway station. Troops set up machine-guns on the roofs of the low buildings at the corners of the square and after a five-minute warning given to the crowd by an officer, began firing. A telegram from the embassy to Kellogg said the military had orders from their commanders not to spare the ammunition and had killed about fifty strikers. Later in the month the embassy revised the estimate to between five and six hundred. The number of soldiers killed was one. A despatch in mid-January 1929 from the embassy to Kellogg reported that the number of strikers killed by the Colombian military exceeded one thousand. This latest headcount came from the United Fruit Company.

The US embassy remarked at the Colombian authorities' unusual zeal in dealing with the problem. It had led to the efficient quelling of the Santa Marta strike, events stirred up by communist ideas and activities, and given way to a state of calm and tranquillity throughout the country. But the embassy was concerned the Colombian press might try to 'inculcate in the popular mind' the idea that the government had been unduly hasty in protecting the interests of United Fruit.

The company was in no doubt that what it had faced in Santa Marta was a 'revolution' of the like seen in Mexico and Russia. Yet within a few days United Fruit employees were back on site at the plantations calmly taking photographs for the company record. Company stores had been inevitable targets, with corrugated roofs torn down, a cash register left charred in the remains and a safe broken open. Some offices and engineers' quarters also lay sacked and burned. A photograph shows Erasmo Coronel's grave with its freshly dug earth and a felt hat laid upon it.

The US gunboat remained an enigma. The Colombian authorities maintained their line that a boat had appeared off shore. The army therefore had had to act against the strikers to spare the humiliation of having US marines land to violate the nation's sovereignty. Critics observed that even supposing the gunboat's presence, there was limited glory in the sovereign republic murdering its own people.

The number of people killed in Ciénaga's plaza was never known. Discussion of their fate was not encouraged by the company or by the Colombian authorities. The popular belief grew up that United Fruit carried their bodies off in railroad cars to unmarked graves in the forest or threw them into the sea.

The story would be told and retold. A few months before the massacre, Gabriel García Márquez had been born in nearby Aracataca. His father was a migrant worker and had not got on with his in-laws. García Márquez's parents moved away from town and he was brought up by his maternal grand-parents.

His grandfather was a retired and respected colonel who had fought in the Thousand Days War. He was a member of the Colombian congress and travelled to it in Bogotá to make a stinging denunciation of the events of Ciénaga while United Fruit and the Colombian authorities made concerted efforts to cover up the affair.

With lessons from the dictionary, García Márquez's grand-father provided some of the boy's education. The old man took him to see the circus when it came to town and, in the stifling heat of the Santa Marta region, to the United Fruit company store to see the 'miracle of ice'. His grandmother was the storyteller, recounting tales of the enclave, of its super-stitions and its ghosts in a deadpan style and as irrefutable truth.

Whatever the details of the massacre, nothing could conceal that it had happened nor contain belief on who had been behind it. A protest six months later in Bogotá prompted a despatch from the US embassy. The occasion was conspicuous, it said, for the number of inscriptions carried by demonstra-tors condemning the government and the army for the way the Santa Marta strike had been put down, and it noted, 'skele-tons and skulls adorned with bunches of bananas were freely displayed'.

7
Banana Republics

It was late 1929 and eighteen years since United Fruit and Sam Zemurray had successfully worked together in mounting their invasion of Honduras. The Banana Man had been little but trouble since. Boston Wasps didn't take to Jews in business, or anywhere, really, and Zemurray didn't take to them.

In the years leading up to the First World War, he and United Fruit had gone to war over their lands that crossed a disputed frontier between Honduras and Guatemala. Or rather, they had prevailed upon the two countries to go to war on their behalf. Zemurray had land on the Honduran side and United Fruit on the Guatemalan. The hostilities had reached such a pitch that Washington had insisted they cool things down as they were causing anti-US feeling in Central America.

The press and analysts of economic affairs liked Zemurray. He didn't seek publicity but, when he got it, it portrayed him in his favoured guise as the small guy pitted against unfavourable odds. Economic experts liked him for similar reasons. His presence as an apparently lone operator bolstered their optimistic beliefs that the system was not condemned to a game between monopolistic giants. The theory of 'The Machine' and efficient monopolies sorting out capitalism to everyone's benefit hadn't really won the hearts of average people. Boom and bust remained the way that the economy worked and the big companies still seemed to emerge on top.

In 1923, Chaim Weizmann, who was seeking to create a groundswell of support for Zionism and a Jewish homeland, had toured the US and asked to visit New Orleans and Zemurray. Weizmann described meeting the Banana Man as one of the highlights of his trip and was struck by his 'unassuming simplicity'. A quarter of a century later, on the foundation of the state of Israel, the wisdom of Weizmann's decision to visit Zemurray would be seen.

Andrew Preston had died in 1924. While he and Minor Keith were the principal architects of United Fruit, Preston's main task had been to run a tight domestic ship. He had built the banana business as it spread across the US in refrigerated railway cars to the Midwest and beyond. As Keith had cut a swathe through Central America, Preston had tended to Washington's growing thicket of anti-trust laws and regulations. He made sure his lobbyists were in place to argue the company's case for freedom from the inherent repression of the state, its red tape and other obstacles to ambitious purpose. He had been largely successful.

Old photographs show a portly Preston, bewhiskered and dressed in Victorian sobriety, alongside his wife in their horse-drawn carriage. They were the understated celebrities of Swampscott, just along the north shore from Boston. From humble fruit importer on Boston's Long Wharf, who had brought in the first full shipload of 'Yellows' in 1871, Preston had risen and 'made it'. He had had a number of fine houses built or remodelled that were the grandest around. Yet Swampscott wasn't quite Marblehead, the nearby home of old money. As much as Preston hobnobbed with the best families, the Cabots, Lodges and the rest, in the Algonquin and their other sombre clubs, the invisible inner sanctum of

Brahmins was full. United Fruit's president had died in eminence but without his family quite becoming 'the Prestons'.

United Fruit had extended a helping hand to Coca-Cola. Based in provincial Atlanta, the brown fizz business was only chugging along after the latest slump of the early 1920s. Coca-Cola's owners had even wondered whether the company was worth keeping alive before the step was taken to explore a new frontier. United Fruit started bottling Coca-Cola in Guatemala where there was no better place for the sugary drink than the draining humidity of the plantations. The company handed it out to its workers and got them hooked. Coca-Cola went on sale in United Fruit's stores, towns and beyond, and more joint ventures followed. From bashful enclave beginnings, Coca-Cola made its way into the world.

The pressing issue became Minor Keith and his railways. The one-time jungle colossus was in his eighties: 'an apple-headed little man with the eyes of a fanatic', according to one quite friendly business source. Keith finally wanted to retire and, if there was one thing he and United Fruit had long been fanatical about it was keeping the banana and railway sides of things separate in strict legal terms. Different companies ran each side of the business. Everyone knew they were one and the same, yet technically they were not. With the driving force of Keith around, it was difficult to imagine the railways belonging to anyone else. With him gone, they would be at risk of takeover. Vultures circled from Britain and Germany, keen railway nations.

United Fruit had decided to absorb Keith's railroads. The monopoly implications were likely to attract anti-trust lawyers, although they tended not to get involved till invoked by some greater power. This was no mere business issue, after all, but strategic and concerning 'interests'. The State Department was charged with the magisterial vision of the wider world and accepted the company's idea. The department had no wish to see such a valuable commodity as Keith's railways fall into the hands of foreigners.

United Fruit's stock market advisers planned a public announcement of the new ownership arrangements. It would be just the thing for market confidence and would deter foreigners with takeover notions. The board of United Fruit disagreed. Its members were old money, with sensible discretion preferred. Announcements were kept to a minimum.

Keith's New York lawyers took charge of the case. Robert Lansing, his old legal counsel and former secretary of state had retired and Keith engaged Lansing's nephews, John Foster Dulles and his brother Allen Dulles. John Foster was well known to United Fruit for arguing the company's case for dictatorship in Costa Rica to President Woodrow Wilson at the time of the First World War. Wilson had not listened but John Foster had moved on. He and his brother Allen were successful lawyers and partners in their firm and were destined for high public office in about twenty years' time. More immediately they had a talent for secrecy and for mastering a complex brief. The affairs of United Fruit and Keith's railway involved a mass of intertwined contracts and arrangements that the Dulles brothers came to know arguably better than United Fruit and Keith themselves.

Thus at peace, in June 1929 Minor Keith slipped quietly from this earth, so much of which he had owned. On Broadway he had briefly engaged in menswear, moved on to lumber, cattle and Costa Rica, where he had kept turtles and the company store with limited success. Having nearly lost faith, he had been persuaded to stay on, whence he prospered. He died the 'uncrowned king of Central America'.

Keith had been Zemurray's mentor and the Banana Man had chosen this time of leadership changes at United Fruit to rejoin battle over the lands on the Honduran and Guatemalan border. He had miscalculated. Previously Honduras was his bastion and he had been candid about the extent to which he had its politicians in his pocket. 'A mule,' he had said, 'costs more than a Honduran deputy.' United Fruit had since taken this advice and out-manoeuvred him with its superior cash flow. The level of bribes in the Honduran capital, Tegucigalpa at this time, prompted a debate in the US capital itself, with Congress finally agreeing that it was just how business was done 'down there'. In so doing, United Fruit had made it its business to secure water rights on the disputed border. Irrigation became impossible for Zemurray and his humiliation inevitable, as he had trailed up to Boston to tender United Fruit his apologies for causing such trouble.

United Fruit had concluded that Zemurray would continue to cause trouble, however, and that the only one way to stop him was to take him over. The company took soundings from the State Department on whether this might attract the attention of the anti-trust lawyers over at the Department of Justice. The State Department had indicated no need for concern and accepted United Fruit's idea that a merger would be good for peace in Central America.

Zemurray was reluctant to get involved again with what he regarded as the evil giant. This was until United Fruit had one of its chief board members eventually catch up with him in November 1929 in a pub in the City of London. They agreed to form a new United Fruit, in which Zemurray would be the main shareholder and have a place on the board but would have no role in the day-to-day running of the company. The price was thirty-three million dollars, with the deal signed over twelve bottles of Bass. The Banana Man was apparently the tipsier of the two. He had agreed that nearly all the payment to him was to be in shares in the new company. The fact that the New York markets had crashed just a few weeks before in October seemed to have escaped his mind.

An even larger giant was born. The new United Fruit extended across three million acres, or 12,000 square kilometres. As one observation had it, United Fruit dwarfed 'the planet's smallest half dozen countries combined'. In US terms, its size was half as much again as the combined areas of the states of Rhode Island and Delaware and marginally less than that of Connecticut. United Fruit had become the un-starred state on the US flag.

Zemurray went off to tend his azaleas. On his Tangipahoa parish estate near New Orleans he plotted a trail for them through the forest of magnolia, cypress and gum. This was not exactly the jungle he was used to but he was tired of living in small, screened settlements along the Mosquito Coast. He enjoyed reading and in Central America the books in his library had only grown mould. He wanted to educate his two children in the US. In Louisiana he could walk out through the ante-bellum columns of his home and stroll around his lake that mirrored the cast-bronze statues at its edge. Zemurray had a hunting lodge in the pine woods and shot quail. With his wife he travelled to New York to take in the shows and, at last, he could enjoy his wealth. It was just a shame that the wealth was fast disappearing.

United Fruit measured its annual prosperity in standard ways: stems exported, bunches sold, prices on the stock market board. What might be termed its 'machete index' was more informal though a useful rule of thumb. In the realm of big knives, United Fruit was the largest machete buyer in the world. Each of its plantation labourers, *mozos*, 'peasants', had to have one purchased from the company store. United Fruit itself bought them from the Collins Company of Collinsville, Connecticut, the 'world's greatest machete maker'. English and German models were cheaper but United Fruit was a down-home New England firm. Collins's three salesmen sweated their way around the region with their heavy samples cases, jumping on and off riverboats and labouring along plantation trails. In a good year, they sold United Fruit 36,000 machetes. Yet in 1931 during the Depression, the company bought only 24,000, a reduction in demand of a third.

Zemurray's fortune collapsed more dramatically. Shares worth thirty-three million dollars at the time of the merger slumped in value to two million. He also faced other, more political threats. Louisiana governor Huey Long, the 'Kingfish', had him in his sights. Long was a swampland populist with a thing about fascism. He was the 'small man's' man, but not Sam's kind of man. He had swept to power after the Mississippi flood of 1927 when the grandees of New Orleans had allowed the deluge of poor areas of town in order to save their own. Though the governor had never professed much of an interest in foreign affairs, lately he seemed to have found one. US marines had engaged these many years in fighting wars in Central America, he said, for 'that corrupt banana peddler Zemurray'.

The Banana Man took to pacing the New Orleans waterfront

with a dwindling bank account and no power base. He spoke to captains of the Great White Fleet, more jaundiced by the day. They sailed up from Central America with holds half full. They had to cut back on oil, slow their journeys and risk what cargo they had going rotten.

Zemurray wrote to United Fruit's board, buzzing with suggestions. The Wasps ignored him. When he travelled to Boston for a shareholders' meeting the top table professed not to understand a word he was saying because of his Russian accent. For the time being, he withdrew but quietly proceeded to win the support of other discontented shareholders. In early 1933, he attended the next quorum of the board. It had just finished a discussion on irrigation in Honduras. Everyone had previously agreed that he would not intervene in such mundane company matters but no one had said anything about his taking United Fruit over. Zemurray skimmed his collection of share certificates and majority voting rights down the long polished oval table, announcing in guttural yet graspable tones: 'You gentlemen have fucked this company up long enough.'

With Zemurray's takeover, the United Fruit story acquired a new dimension in colour. The Banana Man was good copy for journalists. United Fruit had been stuck in its narrow mentality, a sealed unit. It released information such as short histories of the banana and recipes for its use. In 1929 it had also created its 'education department' to get teaching packs into schools. United Fruit, whether through the Boston blue-bloods in their clubs or the supervisors on its plantations, kept itself cut off until such time as it chose to communicate.

Zemurray welcomed the press attention, possibly as a means of deflecting the predatory tendencies of Governor Long. East-coast journalists headed south to New Orleans to absorb the atmosphere of the Big Easy: the 'greatest banana port in the world'. Strapping dockworkers, 'Negroes, Maltese, Italians', worked in an air 'pungent with smells from every land'. After the scribes had journeyed with the Great White Fleet to arrive in Central America, their impressions became less sanguine.

It was a tough world. Male expatriates drank whisky to deter diseases of one kind or another. Back home they had been good clean boys who had gone off to learn about management. In Central America they carried .38s to protect themselves from the workforce. Drunk on payday, a machete-wielding *mozo* was dangerous enough but what happened if one of those guns fell into his hands? Labourers' quarters were positioned beyond shooting distance of overseers' houses. In the event of disputes there was also an unwritten code that was not exactly the due process of law: if a *mozo* killed a *mozo* he'd be moved to another farm; if a white man killed a *mozo* he'd be sent to another country; if a *mozo* killed a white man he'd be 'accidentally shot'.

One description of a United Fruit banana division spoke of a 'vast feudal estate' composed of drab artificial settlements similar to factory towns. Labour camps, long lines of miserable and hot bunkhouses stood next to smoky railway yards and noisy machine shops. United Fruit's company areas resembled boom towns that, as banana cultivation deteriorated and moved on, became the 'decadent villages' that had marked the US's industrial expansion of the nineteenth century. So this was progress. And there was no anti-trust thinking here. All power was centred on the 'great corporation'. United Fruit decided everything, not least the shade of paint on its trim business quarters: a 'malarial yellow', some called it.

There was a brighter side. The plantations' expatriate workers had beaches and bridle paths, pools or offshore diving bells to enjoy. In Honduras, Tela was a garden spot, with a new golf course manicured by goats. Twenty-five miles away Trujillo had its Spanish fort, against whose wall William Walker, would-be King of Nicaragua, had met his end in the 1860s. More pleasant was the nearby port of Puerto Castilla, United Fruit's pride and joy that had been developed from nothing. It had a yacht club and its own jazz band, bow-tied and in starched cuffs, the 'Banana Six'.

Journalists' attentions wandered as the 'seasoned fruit men' who showed them around wanted to talk about the fine alkaline soil of the northern Honduran coast and how it was not susceptible to disease. But what was that over there? An expanse of 'sere, yellow trees', acres and acres of them. And was it true that in Bocas del Toro in Panama the Great White Fleet wasn't letting passengers off to sightsee because of the visible effects of disease? Well, yes, but Bocas del Toro was always a dump anyway.

Zemurray's experiment with the press proved to be a disaster. United Fruit's world was going rotten. In the Central American region, banana disease had claimed a total of one hundred thousand acres. Honduras had an area under banana cultivation of ninety-six thousand. United Fruit had lost the equivalent of Honduras.

United Fruit had been warned. In the late 1920s, when Panama disease had finally arrived in Honduras, the people from the US Department of Agriculture had also turned up. Their findings were no more welcome than they were. Monoculture was not working and banana production was out of 'equilibrium'; alternative crops were needed. Honduras had been the last to succumb to Panama disease but in the mid-1930s became the first territory hit by sigatoka. The two diseases combined to disastrous effect and where the life of a plantation at the turn of the century had been up to ten years, now it was less than three. The company departed from vast areas and in 1935 even abandoned Puerto Castilla.

The manner of United Fruit's retreat was, in itself, disastrous. Jobs, livelihoods and whole communities vanished. United Fruit ripped up railway tracks and threw them into the ocean. This was wanton destruction; what purpose could possibly be served? Bridges were dismantled, their wooden supports left to rot by the sides of rivers. Any materials United Fruit wanted to keep for itself it loaded on trucks and was gone.

What was it doing about the people it left behind? Nothing. What was it doing about the diseases that had caused this problem? Nothing. Did the company want to do anything about disease? Perhaps such affliction was to its commercial advantage because it deterred potential competitors. Why would United Fruit expend vast amounts on research into disease control if rivals stepped in to reap the reward?

United Fruit's response when disease had taken hold was to move on to new land, to a new country if need be, and to carve out another part of Central America's infinite jungle. As the thought began to occur that perhaps the jungle was not so infinite anymore, Zemurray finally addressed the problem. He found a solution, which was called 'Bordeaux Mixture' and that combined copper sulphate, water and lime. Zemurray's experts cautioned him against its overuse but he had it pumped on the plantations in increasing quantity. It was a cocktail with quite a pleasant name, but the giveaway was in the title of those employed to spray and pump it: *veneneros*, or for want of a better translation, 'poisoners'.

United Fruit's annual reports and meetings did not dwell on the negatives. Disease didn't 'sell'. Besides, in the mid-1930s things were looking up for the company as the Depression began to lift. The advertising industry had helped by recently redefining the popular symbol of household wealth. This had previously been the 'full dinner pail'. The term was thought too closely identified with the working class, and depressing given how many people were out of work. The new cheerier symbol was to be the 'full cereal bowl' and would prove far more useful to United Fruit. Bananas would yet burgeon in the breakfast bowls of the nation.

In Central America United Fruit kept moving. Its retreat from disease looked like a rampaging advance. Under Keith and Preston, production had migrated west from the Caribbean islands to Central America. Now United Fruit pointed the banana further in the direction of the setting sun.

In Guatemala the company had had land for a long while on the Pacific side of the isthmus. It had not used it and, as usual, kept it mainly to ward off competitors. Those that tried to compete had either been put out of business by the freight rates charged them on Keith's railway, or by United Fruit purchasing the favours of whichever dictator was in power.

The latest was General Jorge Ubico, who was a man of pride and bearing. He compared himself to Napoleon, had his nose and affected a Bonaparte hairstyle. In the world of ideas he despised Hitler as a lower-class upstart and was a disciple of Mussolini. Anyone who could bring discipline to such a people as the Italians, he contended, had lessons for the Guatemalans. In United Fruit, General Ubico had a party that made the railways run on time while he applied firm direction from the centre. The fortunate few Guatemalan children who attended school were clad in military uniform. He chose the music for the national symphony orchestra and progressed on speaking tours of the country accompanied by piped bands. Most of those coerced into the nation's plazas to listen were Guatemala's Mayan majority who did not speak Spanish and had no idea, nor cared, what he said.

Ubico would not listen to the pleas from his oligarchy to stop United Fruit's spread to the Pacific: the company set up its complex of plantations on the Pacific at Tiquisate. It was state of the banana-art with the latest in irrigation and other technology, above all the powerful pumps that delivered Bordeaux Mixture in the volume thought necessary.

In the Pacific coastal lowlands, no less hot than those on the Atlantic, Tiquisate had well-appointed expat housing on concrete pylons to allow the flow of air and to guarantee the continuing flow of young Americans coming for purposes of character reinforcement. 'New employee's home: Engineer Bump' read the caption on the proud company photo of one such two-storey structure to be used by young engineer Almyr Bump, recently arrived in Tiquisate from the US.

A cartoon appeared in a local magazine to mark the arrival of United Fruit. It showed the isthmus straddled by a grinning tentacled monster. From Atlantic to Pacific its reach was everywhere and United Fruit would never shake off this image of *El Pulpo*, 'the octopus'.

The *Oxford English Dictionary* (OED) cites 1935 as the year when the term 'banana republic' first came into use. A fictional tale in the July issue of *Esquire* magazine had included a conversation between two of its characters and a retired military figure, an ancient-mariner type who had grabbed their attention: 'We strung along with Major Brown on the inhuman aspects of war in the banana republics.'

O. Henry's *Cabbages and Kings* had actually beaten *Esquire* by thirty-odd years but it was fair to say that by now the term had a new meaning. The republics of Central America were less the cheery haunts of O. Henry, Lee Christmas and Machine-gun Molony than the benighted locales of United Fruit.

In the depths of Depression in the first half of the 1930s, Central America had sunk to a new level of dependency on United Fruit. The states borrowed money from the company to keep national budgets afloat. Meanwhile, the company reduced its dependence on them. United Fruit looked elsewhere to diversify and in Africa, for example, it grew African palm for the manufacture of palm oil.

Banana republics became characterised as places of inhuman wars and dictatorships, which was not altogether far from the truth, but now the term implicitly disparaged their inhabitants for succumbing. Conversely the protagonists came out of it rather well. Commentary from the US, if made at all, came from a position of assumed superiority.

At home, United Fruit inspired awe. Its 'contact man' pulled the strings in all Central American capitals, wrote *Fortune* magazine: 'If the finance minister were to overdraw his account, or the archbishop wanted six nuns transported from Germany; if the president's wife wanted her gallstones removed, or the minister's wife liked fresh celery from New Orleans, or the president wanted three blooded cows served by a blooded bull; if anyone wants almost anything, then United Fruit's "contact man" is the one who can quickly get it.'

Also at this time, the OED made its reference to another new turn of phrase: 'going bananas'. It meant a developing state of derangement and was peculiarly in tune with what had been happening.

As President Franklin D. Roosevelt attempted to pull the US out of Depression, a band of US business moguls had picked up on United Fruit's wackier ideas. They objected to Roosevelt's New Deal. His programme entailed a lot of expensive plans to build bridges across San Francisco Bay and other such schemes to get unemployed US citizens back to work. The moguls believed in the prevailing economic theory that you left well alone; for that matter, you left 'bad' alone, too. It would cure itself. In the ways of the jungle, the weakest went under and the most able survived, leaving everyone better off. As for Roosevelt's ideas, they were costing a lot of taxpayers' money and since so many ordinary taxpayers were out of a job more of the burden fell on the moguls and big companies. Some of them had resolved to put a man more to their own liking in the White House. They did not conspire to throw Roosevelt out completely, but to have their man work alongside him in order that he might see sense.

Their plan was to make a banana republic of the US. They had chosen their own 'Major Brown' figure and he 'strung along' with them for a while. He was Brigadier General Smedley D. Butler and he had the right credentials. He was a retired marine with thirty-three years' service in Central America.

Alas for the plotters, he knew too much about the inhuman aspects of Central America's wars. 'For the benefit of Wall Street,' he wrote in his book, *War is a Racket*, 'I helped in the rape of half a dozen Central American republics.' Butler turned state's evidence, claiming a cabal of bond salesmen, bankers and industrialists wanted to overthrow the president and take the US to war. He alleged the involvement of famous names, among them J. P. Morgan, the bankers, but many others besides. Butler took his claims to Washington and the House of Representatives' Un-American Activities Committee. It accepted his story. 'There was no doubt that General Butler was telling the truth,' the committee's co-chair later recalled.

Yet the affair blew over and before long few people would remember it at all. The plotters dismissed Butler's claims as fanciful madness: 'moonshine'. President Roosevelt, meanwhile, knew that if his New Deal was to get the money it needed it would require a deal with big business. As later events showed, Roosevelt was also at odds with what he saw as Butler's looney anti-war isolationism. The brigadier general died a little before Pearl Harbour, consigned quietly to history as having indeed 'gone bananas'.

In the build-up to the Second World War, Sam Zemurray engaged in his own opposition to Roosevelt. The Banana Man did not agree with the president's wishes for Central America. In overseas affairs Roosevelt had his 'Good Neighbor' policy designed to develop good relations between the two halves of the American continent. The idea was that the US would buy more of Latin America's raw materials, bananas included. In return, Central America and Latin America in general would buy more US manufactured goods. This mutual arrangement would promote economic recovery.

To swing the process along, the northern half of the Americas imported Carmen Miranda, the Brazilian song and dance star. Though scantily clad by the standards of the north, she was hardly raw talent. She wowed the crowd in her opulent tutti-frutti hat and for a while things seemed to go rather well.

Sight for sore eyes that Carmen Miranda was for those who had endured so many depressing years, she didn't fit with United Fruit's view. There were other 'Good Neighbors' with whom to do business, although they were a little further away. Over in Europe, Hitler's Germany was vigorously re-arming and industrialising. Germans were getting wealthier and were a very good market for bananas. The Nazis would only pay in bonds exchangeable for German manufactured goods, so United Fruit needed Central America to take as many of those products as possible. With transport costs, however, they might be more expensive than similar goods from the US.

United Fruit decided to see what it could do. In Guatemala it controlled the rates charged to have goods sent as freight by rail. These rates went through curious contortions, such that German goods proved remarkably cheap in the market place compared with their counterparts from the nearby US. United Fruit's business with Hitler boomed.

President Roosevelt was furious. Rather than helping the US's economic recovery, United Fruit had chosen to assist Germany's revival under the Nazis. As the US prepared to enter the Second World War, it viewed United Fruit as a hostile power and a second Roosevelt put anti-trust investigators on the company's case.

8
On the Inside

United Fruit worked its way into the heart of US life, into the family and the affairs of state and, when it mattered most, into the State Department.

Since 1929 United Fruit's education department had engaged in grabbing its audience while it was young. It sent maps for school geography lessons and pictures for kids to colour. Its 'home economics department' supplied a flow of material for mums. The ubiquitous sliced banana with cereal each morning became such a feature that some kids grew up believing the two just came that way. The fruit was certainly better suited to slicing on the morning cereal than apples were. United Fruit also harboured hopes that banana bread could outdo 'apple pie'. Here the apple held firm, banana bread being far too heavy to displace it in the nation's affections.

Winking bananas on the covers of booklets promised 'new tempting ways' to serve them: 'bananas and bacon', United Fruit suggested; chunks of the fruit wrapped and served on a cocktail stick were 'guaranteed to start a conversation'; 'serve them in some fashion – cooked or raw – at all meals', ordered the company. This was, perhaps, wishful thinking given that hardly anyone outside the Caribbean knew how to cook bananas, and generally no one imported the type of banana suited to cooking anyway.

United Fruit's pictures of Boy Scouts smiling round the campfire and throwing bananas in to be cooked gave the right impression of the company as one with the pillars of civil order. Its posters had bananas marching around like soldiers. Yet United Fruit wasn't above messing with established protocols. Good mums enforced the rigid routine of three meals a day if possible and with nothing between them – 'you'll spoil your dinner'. But United Fruit sidled into the kitchen suggesting that the health-laden banana was above all that: it wasn't enough just to have it at 'all meals' anymore; why not all day? 'Give them to the kiddies', the company said, '"between times".'

United Fruit lived in a world of its own, both real and imagined, called 'Banana Land'. It made programmes about it for the popular medium of the day, such as 'Radio Bound for Banana Land'. Magazines picked up on the idea and promoted it. Short stories of minor intrigue were set on banana plantations, where men in high boots met scantily clad women. Dangerous work combined with easy living, with iced bourbon and inner reflections on the veranda when the day was done. The imperial British had Somerset Maugham in the Far East, sweating in the rubber of 'Malaya'. United Fruit had Banana Land, somewhere down in the mystical south.

A fortunate few had been there. They went on the Great White Fleet from New Orleans to Cuba and beyond. Some Honduran ports were a little flea-bitten. Puerto Barrios in Guatemala was the worst, with its broken paths, ditches full of sewage ebbing and flowing with the tide. Did it ever go away? How did the people live in their corrugated tin and cardboard hovels? You'd never have imagined it like this on the radio. Forty miles inland at Guatemalan company HQ in Bananera, things decidedly improved. Spic-and-span offices had well-dressed young men at desks and whirring wooden fans on the ceiling. The company had its excellent hospital at Quiriguá; it showed how United Fruit was 'there to help'. The company didn't let you get off at Almirante Bay in Panama but then, nor did you want to. There were always those nights in Havana to remember: the 'mulatto' women, and men, too. Such shows, such things that you wouldn't mention when you were back home again.

During the Second World War no one went anywhere on the Great White Fleet's usual run. Many of its number were put to service and many were lost. At the onset of the war President Roosevelt had withdrawn his anti-trust people from United Fruit's case. The deal was that the company would use some of its plantations to grow strategic materials, like rubber, quinine and abaca for rope. Sam Zemurray was put on the board that supervised the programme. Although United Fruit had gone into the conflict as an enemy of the state, it came out of it a bloodied war hero.

Throughout the war United Fruit prepared for peace. Zemurray had become increasingly concerned about the company's image as the 'evil octopus' and around the outbreak of war he had hired Edward Bernays to improve it. Bernays was the 'Father of Public Relations'. He had had a head start: he was a nephew of Sigmund Freud and adept in the new discipline of psychoanalysis. In 1917 he had arranged a tour of the US for the 'Great Caruso', the Italian tenor. After the First World War, Bernays had been the US's press and radio liaison at the Versailles peace talks.

In the late 1920s he made a real name for himself with his book, *Propaganda*. Bernays was the first, and possibly the last, public relations person to be so candid about his discipline. Its concern was the 'group mind'. This didn't 'think', he wrote, but instead had impulses, habits and emotions. The key was for some force to harness them. The force was propaganda, or 'the conscious and intelligent manipulation of the organised habits and opinions of the masses'. This process of manipulation was an 'unseen mechanism of society' and those that made use of it were an 'invisible government' and the 'true ruling power of our country'. Of course, by the 1940s propaganda had long been abused by Stalin in Russia and Hitler in Germany, but Bernays was not deterred or embarrassed. The 'intelligent minority' of US society needed to use propaganda 'continuously and systematically'. This, he asserted, was for the 'progress and development of America'.

Bernays stressed the importance of contacts and boasted a long list of them. Many were journalists, senior editors among them, a number of whom he called friends. They were a good conduit for manipulating the organised opinions of the masses and Bernays believed in using them continuously and systematically.

Zemurray had failed when he invited journalists into United Fruit's world in the 1930s and was soon convinced that, with Bernays, he had got it right this time. Bernays breathed on reality, changed it, and yet somehow it was still 'real'. He had a pedigree of commissions from among those who worked society's unseen mechanism. The American Tobacco Company had used him in the good times leading up to the late 1920s crash. American Tobacco wanted more women to smoke more publicly. The problem was they were doing it in the privacy of their own homes, or in dance halls and other enclosed spaces. They weren't smoking enough outside, where it still wasn't 'ladylike'. Bernays conjured a link between cigarettes and a rising sense of women's confidence and liberation. In

1929 he had had female models stride along in New York's Easter Parade smoking, not cigarettes but 'lights of freedom'.

For United Fruit Bernays suggested the company execute what in modern advertising jargon might be called 'repositioning'. Central America, he decreed, would have both a new name and location. It would become 'Middle America'. At home in the US the name conveyed the right image of respectability and good values. As for United Fruit, Middle America was where it would be. Bernays had been impressed by his own travels to this part of the world. He had visited Zemurray in Honduras, in Tela: 'a small seaport town a stone's throw from the jungle'. Bernays remarked how, from the wilderness, Zemurray had built what looked like a 'small Midwest community', with flowers around the pleasant frame houses.

The company set up a 'Middle America Information Bureau'. Bernays declared that United Fruit had thereby 'opened up' to public scrutiny. The bureau provided facts and figures on United Fruit's work to journalists from the US and Latin America. A weekly publication called *Latin America Report* was geared towards businessmen. In charge of it was William Gaudet, 'Bill' to his friends, who was regarded as a 'good friend of the company'. This meant United Fruit and the other 'company', the US Central Intelligence Agency.

Philanthropy was good, Bernays advised. Zemurray had already set up a children's clinic in New Orleans. One million dollars went to the city's Tulane University for 'Middle American' research. A Harvard professorship was created for women. In Honduras, the company opened the first school for the advanced study of agriculture by Central Americans. It was timely, since diseased plantations were closing at such a rapid rate. Bernays advocated United Fruit should put more money into Guatemala's neglected archaeological ruins. The company restored an ancient Mayan ball-game court, an arena in which, it was said, losers had paid the ultimate price. United Fruit emerged the winner as Bernays made sure a commemorative postage stamp was issued.

The approaching end of the Second World War posed challenges. Banana sales had slumped by half during the conflict. They would surely rise when United Fruit's boats could get back to peaceful work on the high seas but by how much? The United States was the only world economy to have escaped the ravages of war intact and looked forward to a postwar boom. It anticipated a surge in demand for substantial consumer goods: more and newer cars, televisions to replace antiquated radios, refrigerators, vacuum cleaners. How could United Fruit harness this upturn?

Advertising was the treasure chest and the key was to tap into people's aspirations and desires. Previously, advertising had concentrated on 'utility', namely on getting people to 'use' more of a given product. The drawback was that there might be a ceiling on how many or how much they thought they could use. Tune into their dreams and it would be quite different. Utility was limiting, desire limitless. The way to sell bananas was by grasping the infinite possibilities of desire.

By now, Carmen Miranda had been enjoying great success. She had had big hits with 'Down Argentine Way' in 1940 and 'That Night in Rio' the following year. She seemed happy to go along with the unofficial political role assigned her. She was everything the US could want from a 'Good Neighbor'. The US was grimly engaged in war on so many fronts: Europe, Asia, the small islands of the Pacific. It was comforting to know it had been worth it and Miranda's spirit seemed to speak for an appreciative outside world.

United Fruit happened upon the cartoon character of Señorita Chiquita Banana. Shaped as a banana she danced and sang in her ruffled Latin dress and fruit-strewn hat. Songs and advertising jingles were crafted around her, sheet music was sent to schools. Radio, cinema and all the new TVs spread the message. One US radio station played her jingles 657 times in one day. US troops posted abroad voted Chiquita the 'woman' with whom they'd most like to share a foxhole. To housewives she was vibrancy, good health and perfect teeth, qualities for the new postwar family. Sales soared as Señorita Chiquita Banana captured the exuberance and optimism of the world's sole superpower.

Sam Zemurray aimed to go out on a high note. His bananas symbolised capitalism: small luxuries that led to far more. Communism promised only the dullest in utility and even failed to deliver that. With his world set on the path to fortune and fun, Zemurray decided to retire again. In so doing he planned to reconcile with his roots and old enemies.

No reference books on Jewry in the US South mentioned him and his role in US entrepreneurship. Maybe he preferred it this way. He wore 'no conspicuous prominence on his sleeve,' the rabbi of the New Orleans synagogue he attended later recalled. On the other hand Zemurray had appreciated that visit by Chaim Weizmann, Zionism's missionary, twenty-five years before. They had shared an interest in mathematics and music and, as an escapee from Russian anti-Semitism, Zemurray had found himself inspired by Weizmann's message. So in the late 1940s he helped fund and organise the purchase of the *Exodus*, the boat that would take migrants to the emerging state of Israel.

Zemurray had no obvious successor as company chief. He had never taken to Boston. He could have made an elegant home of any of the brownstones in the Back Bay but preferred the long-term rental of a suite in the staidly grand Ritz-Carlton, overlooking the Common. At such times as he'd needed to recover 'lost energies', he had retreated to New Orleans to fast for days, weeks it was claimed, on water alone.

Zemurray had never apparently sought the acceptance of the Brahmins, however, he had good sense recognising that they ran Boston and that it would be as well for one of them to run United Fruit. If he had been looking for someone of the right blood, he didn't go for half measures; he chose a Cabot.

Thomas Cabot was a pleasant enough fellow. His later autobiography had a friendly foreword from Robert McNamara, President John F. Kennedy's national security adviser at the time of the 1962 Cuban missile crisis. Before that McNamara had reorganised the Ford Motor Company. Old Henry Ford had borrowed United Fruit's mass-market ideas but lingered too long and McNamara had been hired to save the company. Zemurray worried that he, like Ford, had stayed too long but thought he saw something in Cabot that would produce success.

Cabot appeared as effortless old money. Scott Fitzgerald would have admired and despised his jaunt through the decades, with horse-riding and travel. He did have an industrial background, with his side of the family owning carbon-black factories that belched smoke over rolling hills in Pennsylvania. Cabot had run them, not in a manner to leave him exhausted but he seemed to know some of the arts of management.

United Fruit's managers failed to agree. When Cabot took over he did reveal some very interesting ideas. Give up Central America, he said, because it was lost to disease. He wasn't far wrong. Big Mike was close to extinction. Cabot suggested United Fruit should relocate distantly south across the Andes: perhaps that would keep the bugs away. New banana lands were opening up in Ecuador where there would not be the problem of workers organising themselves into unions. In Central America the unions had been getting stronger.

Cabot clashed with deep vested interests. Central America was the company and virtually all it knew. When he went further to say he could not see the point of Bernays' PR, he was considered to be quite out of touch with reality. Zemurray came out of retirement again and sacked him.

The postwar optimism had turned as the Cold War had frozen into uneasy stalemate in Asia and Europe. When the Russians exploded their nuclear bomb in 1949 the US was no longer the only superpower. Carmen Miranda's career had peaked in the war years with *The Gang's All Here* and had taken a decidedly downward turn. Since Roosevelt's death near the end of the war, the US had had enough of 'Good Neighbor'.

Were there any 'Good Neighbors'? One-time allies were unreliable, as the Russians had proved. Communism occupied the eastern half of Europe and threatened the western half. Even Britain was under suspicion. It had voted out Winston Churchill, of all people, after the war, in favour of the Labour government led by Clement Attlee. His strange regime professed 'Social Democracy' and what did that mean beyond a shipload of bananas? It was at least half way to Communism, if not more.

Hollywood came under special scrutiny. Ronald Reagan, the head of the screen actors' union, appeared before the House of Representatives' Un-American Activities Committee to confirm its worst suspicions. Communists were everywhere, agreed Reagan, and he'd be happy to help find them. The committee expressed its grateful thanks for such cheerily forthright testimony. From Wisconsin Senator Joseph McCarthy took up the anti-Communist banner and, in the early 1950s, grilled the nation about the enemy within.

United Fruit instinctively sided with 'McCarthyism'. It was a long way from the decencies of Wisconsin in the company's part of Middle America where a lot was going wrong. In Guatemala General Ubico had been thrown out in 1944 and succeeded by elected governments who were picking arguments with United Fruit. Banana disease had been increasing. On the plantations United Fruit had been pumping Bordeaux Mixture at an ever greater rate and when the bananas were loaded aboard ship the mixture's residue was combining with seeping seawater in the holds. The result was that even the Great White Fleet was rotting from the inside.

Costa Rica had shown signs of making a break from banana republicanism. Would it be a case of 'first in, first out'? Thirty years before in 1919, United Fruit had warned President Woodrow Wilson that a strong leader was needed to maintain control. He hadn't listened then, nor did he when given the same advice by John Foster Dulles, the bright young lawyer who had been doing, in the company's view, some good undercover work in the country. Since then Costa Rica had gone from bad to worse and become steadily more democratic. Its latest leader, José 'Pepe' Figueres, was a real conundrum. He had banned the Communist party, which was as it should be. Then he had abolished the army and turned its barracks into a fine arts museum. Figueres was another one who claimed to be a Social Democrat. This wasn't the Central America United Fruit knew or very much loved.

Company anxiety rose all the more as Guatemala leaned towards more radical leaders. In 1951 the country elected Colonel Jacobo Arbenz, a 'military moderniser'. He was a science and history teacher at the military academy and, as a student, had been one of the academy's brightest graduates. Coming from Quezaltenango in the Indian highlands, Arbenz knew the miserable living and working conditions of Guatemala's Mayan population very well and resolved to improve them.

His wife dominated him, or so it was said. His reedy speaking voice was cited as proof. Señora María Vilanova de Arbenz was charismatic and, possibly, another Evita Perón in the making. It was also suggested that she might have been from the Lady Macbeth mould; she was ambitious and knew something about power.

The president's wife was from El Salvador, Guatemala's next-door neighbour. Minor Keith had run a branch line from his Guatemalan railway to El Salvador, in order to take advantage of its lucrative export trade in coffee but there had not been much scope for bananas. El Salvador was on the Pacific, had no Atlantic coastline and so was not the Central American banana's first port of call. It was a country the size of Massachusetts or Wales and grew mainly coffee, sugar and cotton. El Salvador did have an oligarchy, a very rich one, known as the 'Fourteen Families'. The 'Fourteen' shared United Fruit's worldview and ruled with the military, often corruptly. Elections, if held, were apt to be fixed. El Salvador was like Nicaragua: a 'banana republic' that didn't have very many bananas.

Señora Arbenz was from a privileged background. The Vilanova family was one of the 'Fourteen', though she was an acknowledged black sheep. Well educated, she had upped and gone travelling, uncharacteristic for a well-bred Salvadorean girl. She had lived in Mexico, with its revolutionary tradition, and was well read. When she had married Arbenz, she came with a substantial dowry, a plantation in Guatemala owned by her parents.

Arbenz had announced that he was to carry out a land reform and the Arbenzes made their plantation part of the plan. The reform's aim was to break up a number of large landholdings and distribute small areas to landless farmers. Most of the land United Fruit had to give up had been unused and was part of its stock of territory kept in reserve. When Arbenz said the purpose of breaking up large unproductive landholdings was to pull the Guatemalan economy out of 'feudalism' and to turn it into a 'modern capitalist state', United Fruit and his other enemies angrily dismissed his claims. He was going in for nothing more than words and gestures, which, they said, were to cover his plot to implant Communism. The company was not the only large landholder to be affected but none other had quite the same power base. United Fruit prepared for war.

From his posting in neighbouring Mexico, CIA agent Howard Hunt took a keen interest in Guatemala. He would later claim credit for the clandestine activities that led to the fall of the Arbenz government. It was replaced by decades of military dictatorship during which scores, if not hundreds of thousands of people died as death squads killed or 'disappeared' anyone regarded as politically dangerous. The death squads recruited off-duty or ex-military people and had such names to imply virtue as the White Hand and the Guerrillas of Christ the King. Hunt proceeded to stage botched efforts like the Bay of Pigs invasion of Cuba and, in 1972, the burglary at the Watergate hotel in Washington that brought down the man whose cause it was intended to enhance, the then US president, Richard Nixon. Hunt later wrote novels and also a book with his boss, Allen Dulles, the former lawyer for United Fruit and the head of the CIA's undercover operations. They called their book *The Craft of Intelligence*.

Early CIA reports on Arbenz had referred to him as 'brilliant' and 'cultured'. Hunt revised the intelligence agency's study of the Guatemalan president and declared he was of 'limited intellect'. It would all help build the case that Arbenz's wife dominated him.

At the time, however, the case against Arbenz did not advance. United Fruit lobbyists were making little impression in Washington and Hunt thought he spied the problem. The State Department had a gentlemanly diplomat as ambassador in Guatemala who had reported to Washington that there was nothing illegal or especially worrying about what Arbenz was doing, in fact the new president was actually quite likeable. Hunt complained to Allen Dulles, who sympathised but couldn't set any clandestine operation in motion against Guatemala. It would need the approval of the State Department. Fed up, Hunt took a new posting in the Middle East, in Egypt.

United Fruit was convinced the problem went all the way to the top. President Harry Truman had succeeded Roosevelt and, in the company's view, was too preoccupied by such distant Cold War issues as Berlin and Korea. He failed to see that Guatemala was part of the Communists' grander plan. United Fruit had hatched one of its own plans to send guns down to Central America with the Great White Fleet in boxes marked 'Agricultural Equipment'. The intention was for the Somoza family to receive the weaponry in Nicaragua and lead an assault on Guatemala. Truman and the State Department had blocked the exercise.

The US election in 1952 came as a blessed relief. General Dwight D. Eisenhower, a Second World War hero, took over the presidency for the Republicans. No politician, he was a good administrator. In war he had understood when to delegate. In peace he would do the same, except those to whom he gave the authority would make war on United Fruit's behalf.

John Foster Dulles, presently a senator from New York, was handed the State Department and with it responsibility for foreign affairs. His brother Allen was in prime position as head of the CIA. They were two old confidants and advocates of United Fruit and, in its uncanny way, the company had worked itself into the inner circle.

9
Coup

General Eisenhower, popularly know as 'Ike', came to power in January 1953 arguing that President Truman and his departing Democrats had gone 'soft on Communism'. This was most encouraging for United Fruit but Eisenhower still worried the company. There was a question over the president's commitment to Central America. Like Truman before him, he seemed more interested in very distant events.

Ike appeared obsessed by 'Persia'. Britain had got itself into trouble in the country and asked the US for help. Winston Churchill was back in office in London and Eisenhower was disposed to come to the aid of his old wartime comrade. The Anglo–Iranian Oil Company's huge operations on the Persian Gulf had been seized from the British by a new nationalist government. The British contended that Communists were behind this turn of events. The young Shah of Persia had fled the capital, Tehran, and gone to Europe.

The CIA had been on a tight leash during the Truman administration, when relations between the agency and the State Department had been strained. Under the new regime in Washington, coordinated action between the two required only a phone call between brothers, namely secretary of state John Foster Dulles and CIA director Allen.

Allen Dulles chose Kermit 'Kim' Roosevelt to do the job in Persia. A grandson of former President Teddy Roosevelt and nephew of Franklin D., he was reputed to be one of the CIA's top undercover men. Yet in August 1953 that description hardly fitted the tales from Tehran as the Persian nationalists were forced from power. Some reports said Roosevelt rode into the capital atop a tank. The shah soon returned from leading a playboy's life in Europe and his country gradually ceded its old name to become known as Iran. Britain gave up a substantial share of its Iranian oil assets to the US in return for the favour done.

United Fruit took heart from these faraway developments. Perhaps attention could turn to the company's advantage in Guatemala against what it regarded as the renegade regime of President Jacobo Arbenz and his dangerous wife María. If the US, or rather the Dulles brothers, could help the British in the Persian Gulf they could surely back their old client United Fruit in its problems around the Gulf of Mexico.

The Dulles brothers were contrasting characters. John Foster lacked subtlety and was uncomfortable in company. Churchill had likened him to a bull that carried his china shop around with him. He enjoyed trouble, both making it and following it through. No one could doubt that his methods had gained him success, particularly as a lawyer. Even in the Depression of the 1930s, his annual salary had averaged $370,000. Of the two brothers, Allen was the suave one. He owed much of his success to his urbane manner. He was a popular tennis partner and good in any social gathering. Clover, his wife, was in the habit of shopping for expensive jewellery, paid for by her husband as compensation for his dalliances. Allen Dulles usually kept an eye out for the next chance for adventure.

To help substantiate its case in Guatemala, United Fruit had hired John Clements, a former marine with his own public relations company. Edward Bernays, doyen of the profession, was very much at work with his own influential contacts on the company's behalf but his list was liberal by comparison to that of Clements. Clements shared the views of Senator Joseph McCarthy, who was continuing his public campaign to root out Communism in all its alleged forms. Clements had a list of 800 key thinkers of the right. He dashed out a report that he sent to all of them. It acquired the title 'Report on Guatemala' before he widened it to 'Report on Central America'.

The report held that Communism had already gained a foothold in Guatemala. Quick action was imperative as the enemy closed in. The next objective of Arbenz and his regime was to seize the Panama Canal, a vital asset on sovereign US territory. Thus, from Persia to Guatemala, the fight against Communism had suddenly migrated from the desert to the doorstep. The CIA undertook the report's wider distribution and its findings became accepted government thinking.

The Dulles brothers and President Eisenhower agreed that one advantage of a Guatemalan exercise would be addressing the threat posed by Senator McCarthy. He had outraged Ike with his slurs on the character of the president's wartime colleague, General George Marshall, author of the 'Marshall Plan', the aid programme designed to rebuild the countries of Europe after the Second World War. McCarthy had accused Marshall, among others, of accepting the postwar division of Europe between capitalist West and Communist East.

McCarthy was increasingly becoming a victim of alcohol, swapping gossip daily in bars with a gaggle of friendly journalists. And he showed no sign of stopping his accusations after the Republicans took office. He would bemoan Allen Dulles's

CIA and there was no telling where he might stop. President Eisenhower's brother Milton was a respected expert on Latin American affairs who had said the US should champion reform and compete with Communism for the friendship of the poor. The president himself appeared to be under his brother's influence. Ike had stated that the US would not 'lick Communism' in places like Central America 'unless we can put things into the hands of people who are starving to death'. Such thoughts were bound not to impress McCarthy, nor, for that matter, United Fruit.

An operation in Guatemala would enable the administration to make a strong statement about its position on Communism, whether to the country's enemies of that ideology, or to Senator McCarthy and friends. Just how far Communism had gained a hold in Guatemala was far from certain. A friend of the US president had visited the country and written to him to say that, yes, Guatemala had a small minority of Communists but 'not as many as San Francisco'. Nonetheless, with the Cold War apparently stuck and going nowhere from the US point of view, the administration calculated that Communism needed to be sent a signal of firm US intent. If nothing else, it would increase morale at home.

Guatemala had put its head above the parapet and picked a fight with United Fruit at the wrong time. John Foster Dulles called his brother Allen, who in turn called for Kim Roosevelt. He was summoned to the secretary of state's office and offered the job of overthrowing Guatemala's government, as he had that of Persia. Roosevelt turned the opportunity down. For further coups, he told Dulles, the army and the people in the places concerned had to 'want what we want'.

He seemed to be saying that such conditions did not apply in Guatemala. He also noted the secretary of state seemed unruffled by what he had said. As Roosevelt left the office, Dulles leaned back in his chair 'with a catlike grin on his face'.

On assuming office, the Eisenhower administration soon changed its ambassador in Guatemala. It replaced the diplomat who had not perceived President Arbenz to be a threat with a different kind of character. John Foster Dulles appointed Jack Peurifoy, who was hardly 'diplomatic' at all. He wore a green Borsalino hat with a feather and favoured sports jackets and coloured ties. Of medium height and build, Peurifoy swaggered, sometimes with a revolver in his belt: 'pistol packing Peurifoy', wrote his wife, Betty Jane. A 'Star-Spangled Banner kind of guy', said the ambassador of himself.

He was United Fruit's kind of ambassador. At last, there was a 'strong personality' in the embassy, wrote Edward Bernays. This was in his book *The Biography of an Idea*, his later reflections on a life in public relations in which he devoted a chapter to his time working with the United Fruit Company.

Dulles appointed Peurifoy as one way of keeping McCarthy off the State Department's back. In the late 1940s Peurifoy had slipped files on State Department employees to the House of Representatives' Un-American Activities Committee to help its deliberations on Communist infiltration. Among others, this had won the admiration of one of the committee's most active members at the time, Richard Nixon, now Eisenhower's vice-president.

Peurifoy was from a small rural community in South Carolina and his parents had died when he was young. He had had military ambitions until he had to drop out of West Point through ill health. A bout of pneumonia had, in the military's terms, left him with deficient lung-power. In his civilian life it never held him back. Peurifoy's voice could be plainly heard in any room.

He had pulled himself up from the bottom. In Washington in the Depression he cleared snow from where the rich people lived in Georgetown. He became a lift operator in the Senate. Entering the bureaucracy as a clerk, he made quick progress and joined the State Department. After the Second World War, Peurifoy helped organise the San Francisco conference that founded the United Nations (UN), gentler work than that to which he was suited. He was soon sent to Greece to rally the monarchists in the civil war against the Communists and won the tag of the 'butcher of Athens'. On his desk he still kept a photo of the Greek royal family.

Now in his mid-forties, Peurifoy had been aghast when he was first offered the ambassador's post in Honduras. Tegucigalpa was stuck out of the way and Honduras a backwater. It was not good form to decline the post of ambassador but he did. He demanded Guatemala and got it.

He came at the problem directly. When was Guatemala going to 'stop being a bridgehead for Communism?' he demanded of members of the government as soon as he arrived. He had risen from the dusty village streets of the old south with its oak trees and Spanish moss. He spoke no Spanish and possessed no knowledge of Guatemala beyond basics.

After arriving, Peurifoy did employ some delaying tactics and avoided meeting President Arbenz for two months. When the time came it was over dinner. Their wives remained in attendance throughout, since Mrs Arbenz was apparently not one to retire to exchange dress patterns or banana recipes. The ambassador was shocked by her forthrightness. When he had asked why Guatemala had decreed a day of mourning after Stalin's death in 1953, she had replied that the Soviet leader was a war hero like Roosevelt and Churchill. Had her husband been in power, Roosevelt would have had a similar day when he died.

As the evening wore on Peurifoy became incredulous at President Arbenz's persistence in talking about United Fruit's failure to do much for the Guatemalan economy. United Fruit was a small company in US terms, Peurifoy answered, in the manner of one who wasn't there to discuss small business. His concern was the conspiracy of the Communists to grab power.

The awkward dinner party broke up at two in the morning. Arbenz gave Peurifoy his direct telephone number. Peurifoy would never use it. The candle was burning 'slowly and surely', he reported back to John Foster Dulles. It was only a matter of time in Guatemala 'before large American interests' would be forced out completely if pre-emptive action wasn't taken. When asked soon after how dinner had gone with the Arbenzes, the ambassador said the couple would not be on his next 4th of July invitation list.

To United Fruit, the case for a coup was straightforward. In losing some of its land it had been subjected to an act of 'virtual expropriation', claimed Bernays, and theft. The government had paid compensation in bonds, not cash, which was bad enough, but the manner in which the land had been valued was far worse. The government had used the land's 'book value', namely the figure calculated by the company for tax purposes. The company had under-declared the value of the land for years in order to save on its taxes. Now suffering the consequences, it protested that everyone had known the land's value declared for tax was not the true one. It was accepted business practice. So, why had attitudes in Guatemala changed? The only answer was 'Communism'.

As simple as its case was, United Fruit did not have to argue it alone. It counted on help from some of Boston's best families, members of which were in positions of great influence. It was claimed, of course, that their power went further: there was that toast about the Cabots talking 'only to God'. United Fruit did, indeed, have Cabots on its side but would not have to rely just on them for a link to the Almighty.

Henry Cabot Lodge championed the company's case in his role as ambassador to the UN. After the First World War his father and namesake had not been in favour of the League of Nations, forerunner to the UN, in common with United Fruit. One world war and a new peace forum later, the UN was being used to the company's advantage. Cabot Lodge Junior's voice rang out in defence of a business from his home city of Boston that had been so unfairly treated. The Soviet Union responded that the UN Security Council should send observers to Guatemala to look for themselves, thus giving Cabot Lodge the opportunity to nail their devious intent: 'Keep out of this hemisphere,' he told the Soviets, 'with your conspiracies and plans'.

John Moors Cabot was in charge of Latin American affairs at the State Department. He was the brother of Thomas Cabot, who had been the chief executive of United Fruit in the late 1940s until Sam Zemurray had sacked him. Moors Cabot bore no grudge and warned the Guatemalans that the US government was assuming responsibility for the company's claims. United Fruit calculated that it was being cheated out of compensation for its land to the tune of sixteen million dollars and the State Department sent Guatemala the bill.

It was Howard Hunt who intervened to take the company's case to the highest authority. The CIA man had come back from Egypt, which had proved a poor posting. Egypt had recently lost its king, a British-sponsored monarch who had been replaced by Colonel Gamal Abdel Nasser. Nasser was engaged in challenging Britain over its control of the Suez Canal and possibly calling in the Russians. Diverted from these intriguing issues, Hunt had to attend to the affairs of Albania's King Zog. The king had also been recently deposed and was in exile in Egypt. Hunt took care of matters like reclaiming Zog's imported refrigerator when Nasser's customs officials impounded it.

Hunt jumped at the chance of being part of the action in Central America which he had originally advocated. Allen Dulles, his boss, made him head of politics and propaganda for 'Operation Success', the mission to overthrow the Guatemalan government. From an air base in the swamp near Miami, Hunt made secret trips to the interior of Guatemala contacting anti-Arbenz people: churchmen, businessmen and others. He hired a retired American actor and they prepared scripts for fictitious broadcasts to Guatemala from the Voice of Liberation radio station, which the CIA had specially created. The broadcasts were to convey the impression of a country living in terror and at war with itself. Hunt hired Guatemalan exiles for the part and brought women onto the base to keep them company. The ex-actor coached the exiles on how to present the broadcasts.

The question remained, however, of what was to be done about the Guatemalans who had no radios. In distant rural areas of Guatemala, many poor inhabitants would surely be grateful to hear of the plan to overthrow the government of Arbenz. He was almost certainly an Antichrist and, if he wasn't, then his wife was. The people of rural Guatemala, by contrast, were devout people, awaiting a sign.

Hunt approached Cardinal Francis Spellman of New York, who readily accepted the chance to help stop the spread of atheist influences. The cardinal put Hunt in touch with Guatemala's archbishop and bishops, who were also alarmed at the prospect of Communism in their country. They penned a pastoral letter for the people. Hunt had CIA planes drop thousands of copies of it over forlorn areas whose inhabitants would otherwise not have learned of their pending liberation. When they did, the word came from the skies.

Bernays was ahead of the game. He had drip-fed United Fruit's view into the veins of public opinion since it had become clear that Arbenz would come to power. He had his long list of friendly opinion formers which included sub-categories of those even better placed to manipulate society's 'hidden mechanism'. To take care of them meant all else would follow.

The publishers or senior editors of newspapers were first to be approached. Generally they spent their professional lives office-bound and cut off from the journalistic cutting edge. Bernays put them on planes and United Fruit paid their expenses.

They might lodge in one of the pleasant rooms of the Pan-American hotel, elegantly mock colonial with windows looking out on to the hubbub of Zone One, the heart of Guatemala City. Somewhere in the middle distance pandemonium might erupt. It would be far enough away not to alarm them unduly and near enough to reach just as the crowd was dispersing. It was the perfect foreign correspondent's story: a bit of broken glass, a bullet hole and perhaps a lingering whiff of gun smoke in the air. File it as a 'Communist Outrage'.

Bernays kept up the junkets. These tropical 'fact-finding' tours generally headed first for Bogotá in Colombia and took a whirl by air to the Santa Marta plantations on the Caribbean coast. They set north for Panama, Costa Rica and Honduras, all of which were tranquil and at peace with the company's world. The tension rose as they neared Guatemala. On arrival, company men met them: smiling, reassuring men. It had to be admired how well they withstood the pressure. The company men introduced them to others, local people of some social standing, though not from the government. They did their best to keep smiling, not as gamely perhaps as the company men, while they explained the nature of the rising terror. It was fortuitous that all was still quiet, yet there was no mistaking that feeling of war in the air.

Bernays called the stories that appeared 'masterpieces of objective reporting'. There was something in what he said: United Fruit's version of events rose above the usual pettiness of news outlets' subjective persuasions. Liberal or conservative, it didn't matter. The *New York Times*, the *San Francisco Chronicle*, the *Miami Herald*, *Time-Life* magazines, *Newsweek*, the *Christian Science Monitor* – it was almost unfair to single them out. They all went along for the ride. Bernays rigorously denied any suggestion of news manipulation and here, too, he had a point. Thomas McCann, the chief in-house PR man at the time, later wrote *An American Company*, a book about his days at United Fruit. He said it was difficult to make a convincing case for manipulation of the press when the victims had proved 'so eager for the experience'.

What accounted for this complicity? Many journalists saw their trade as reporting the 'facts' presented to them by apparently decent and honest people. Among those with an instinct to probe, there was the fear that they and their editors would have to deal with the likes of Senator McCarthy. Vice-president Nixon, too, was comparably hawkish and a staunch supporter of the Guatemalan operation. For the journalists there was also the potential glory. Many of the older scribes had reported on the Second World War. Guatemala promised to be the next generation's 'story of their lives'. Where the last war had been fought so distantly, this one threatened much closer to home. Thanks to the sharp-eyed attentions of United Fruit, the conflict could even be seen at the very lock gates of the Panama Canal. Well, the company had at least flown them over it.

United Fruit expanded its visual side, in line with advancing technology. It was some time since it had mastered the airwaves, with 'Radio Bound for Banana Land'. It produced a film, *Journey to Banana Land*. 'Travel with us on the Great White Fleet and meet your neighbours in Middle America', read its opening titles. Scenes moved from crashing surf on the Caribbean, to volcanoes and aerial shots of Guatemala City. Contented natives abounded on urban streets or with their mules on company plantations. United Fruit had brought them 'greater purchasing power' and 'twentieth-century living'. The film ran for twenty-one minutes, its concluding scenes from the US itself. They showed family meals, school cafeterias, bananas enjoyed on cereal and in milkshakes. In 1954, the crisis year for Guatemala, *Journey to Banana Land* was in high demand in US classrooms.

Apparent philanthropy remained uppermost in the company's mind. It took out magazine advertisements promoting the Red

Cross. The organisation was only too pleased to get the support. So were the publishers of the magazines, because United Fruit paid well above normal advertising rates. In return, articles appeared promoting the company's vision of 'Banana Land'.

In delicate issues of diplomacy John Foster Dulles led the charge. In March 1954 the secretary of state stayed two weeks in the Venezuelan capital, Caracas, at the conference of the Organisation of American States (OAS). The city was in a state of unrest because a military dictatorship had recently seized power. In protest democratic Costa Rica refused to attend the conference; but Dulles seemed quite at home. Some cajoling of OAS members was required since several had not grasped that Guatemala, one of Latin America's weaker countries, posed such a threat to its 'small neighbours'. The Guatemalan delegate complained that the US was 'cataloguing as Communism' all efforts in Latin America for economic independence and 'intellectual curiosity'. In other words, only one line was allowed and most toed it when the time came to cast the vote for 'positive action' against Guatemala. Costa Rica wasn't present and only Mexico and Argentina abstained. The rest went along with the US position, either happy to do so, or persuaded by Dulles's suggestions that they would face the withdrawal of US aid.

At the UN, Henry Cabot Lodge's ambassadorial efforts had worked well. Then came a blip as the Security Council proposed that it would send observers to the region. As members of the Council, the British and French backed the idea. Churchill happened to be visiting Washington. President Eisenhower resolved to talk 'cold turkey' with his British friend over this unwarranted European intervention in the American hemisphere. Britain and France were presently engaged in imperial wars, the British in Cyprus and the French in Vietnam. They could count on no help from the US, Ike said, if they carried on taking the wrong stance on Guatemala. Britain and France duly withdrew their support for the idea of UN observers in Guatemala and the proposal was quashed.

The question was who would lead the Guatemalan invasion. Colonel Carlos Castillo Armas was an enemy of Arbenz and had been part of an earlier plot to overthrow him. He had fled into exile and, lately, had a career as a furniture salesman in Honduras. Castillo Armas was dapper, moustachioed and had 'that good Indian face', Howard Hunt reported. He would be 'terrific for the people'.

Castillo Armas was a 'little prick', responded the Somozas in Nicaragua, who offered to launch the invasion. The US had provided the Nicaraguan army with the finest military equipment in Central America, which they claimed could easily handle Arbenz's forces. Washington counselled that it would be unwise for a foreign country to be such an obvious presence in the invasion. Cards had to be played far more carefully. The US accepted the Somozas' offer of training camps and an airfield on the Atlantic coast at Puerto Cabezas, the old pirate haven of Bragman's Bluff.

Castillo Armas was housed, fed and watered on a United Fruit plantation on the Honduran side of the border with Guatemala and awaited his call. Eventually, a straggling force of Guatemalan exiles crossed the frontier and began its march on the capital. The CIA's Voice of Liberation radio station reported an army progressing triumphantly and people flocking to join it. The local mule population fell sharply, with slaughtered animals dumped on the road to give the impression of battles fought along the way.

Many journalists were holed up in the bar of the Pan-American hotel. Any who wanted to go to the 'front' were prevented from doing so for their 'own safety'. Gun in belt, ambassador Peurifoy briefed reporters on another point of concern. He had heard that some of them were calling what was happening an invasion and he put them right: it was a liberation. They were only allowed to see for themselves when the battle was finally done and when Castillo Armas, the good Indian, showed his face on the national palace balcony to spontaneous rapture from the crowd.

Earlier CIA planes had dropped bombs on military bases and in the slums of the capital to create panic among the people and uncertainty in the armed forces. President Arbenz had had the impression that security had broken down and that his forces had abandoned him. In his final broadcast to the nation, he blamed United Fruit for the invasion. A handful of people heard him as the CIA worked to jam the transmission.

In Boston, journalists showed little frustration at not being at the frontline. United Fruit kept them so well informed and most were happy with the hospitality and regular updates, as United Fruit appointed itself the news agency of the war. At company headquarters, they were shown pictures of bodies of alleged victims of atrocities by Arbenz's forces. Thomas McCann, there as part of United Fruit's PR machine, later wrote that the pictures could have been of victims from either side, or of one of Central America's many earthquakes.

10
'Betrayal'

Howard Hunt had faced an existential dilemma. Life was far better viewed as a simple division between the guys in the white hats and the guys in the black hats and, for a moment, he had lost his usual clarity. He had, perhaps, been on an airfield outside Guatemala City near one of the ravines at the capital's outskirts, with gentle wisps issuing from the nearby Fuego volcano. Though the details are vague, after a brief and vigorous bout of combat Hunt had captured a rag-tag group of fighters opposed to efforts by the CIA and the United Fruit Company to overthrow the government. Hunt had wondered whether he should shoot the members of this vanquished band or let them go. In victory he chose the path of mercy and later reflected that this had been a disastrous mistake. One of his captives had been Ernesto 'Che' Guevara.

It is difficult to know whether this really happened. Twenty years later, during the administration of President Richard Nixon, a CIA colleague said Hunt had told him the story. Hunt enjoyed putting out false reports and, having made the better part of a career of it, wrote his autobiography, *Undercover: Memoirs of an American Secret Agent,* in which he neglected to mention the Guevara incident. He said he had not been in Guatemala at the time. It was one of his greatest professional regrets as he had done so much of the groundwork to remove the government of the day, the first Communist regime, as

Hunt viewed it, to meet such a fate since General Francisco Franco's victory in the 1930s in Spain. Come the time of triumph in Guatemala, Hunt wrote, the CIA had reassigned him to Japan. Of course, that might not be true either.

There are scattered details of Che Guevara's time in Guatemala. He had left Argentina to tour Latin America and was especially keen to see what was happening in Guatemala under the government of Jacobo Arbenz. As a young doctor, Guevara wanted to get an idea of developments in healthcare. Among his efforts, he applied to work in the hospital of a United Fruit plantation but did not get the job. A short-back-and-sides sort of company, United Fruit might not have liked the cut of his beard. Guevara kept body and mind together in Guatemala with various jobs, including one selling encyclopaedias. The future revolutionary icon thus served in capitalism's frontline as a simple door-to-door salesman.

Guevara had applied to go to the Guatemalan 'front' as the 1954 coup unfolded and the CIA's dead mule brigade had begun its march on the capital. He had access to Arbenz, who turned down the request, suggesting that the appearance of Guevara and other irregular-looking fighters from Guatemala City would panic the regular army into thinking all was lost. Near the end Guevara urged Arbenz to 'take to the hills' and carry on the fight from the Indian Highlands. Guevara helped organise battalions to guard the capital. Their efforts came to nothing and he sought refuge in the Argentine Embassy before being granted passage out of the country.

His first wife, Hilda, later recounted that the coup in Guatemala had convinced Guevara that the only way forward for Latin America was the 'armed struggle'. Guevara was already coming to this conclusion, having observed the working conditions in Chile's copper mines. After the deeds of United Fruit in Guatemala, Guevara set off north to Mexico to join Fidel Castro's forces preparing for their assault on Cuba.

For some months United Fruit had heard rumours that the US Department of Justice was preparing an anti-trust case against the company, to curb its 'monopolistic practices' in Guatemala. The State Department had ordered the Justice Department's lawyers to hold off from formally beginning legal action during preparations for the Guatemalan coup.

In United Fruit's mind such a case was almost too absurd to credit. If the company monopolised anything it was in doing things the right way. In Guatemala it had just fought the battle for the West against the forces of evil and won. United Fruit ruled the world.

Amid the present uncertainty, the company felt reassured by the attitude of the secretary of state, John Foster Dulles. Al Bump, the company's divisional chief in Guatemala, had heard that normality would soon be restored. Bump had risen from being the company's tyro engineer in the 1930s, with a bright airy house on the new Tiquisate plantation, to the battle-worn frontline manager of the company during the recent Guatemalan crisis. Dulles had instructed the US ambassador that United Fruit was to get back its lands confiscated by Arbenz. The secretary of state didn't mention that, as things would work out, the company would have far more taken away by Washington.

CIA agents descended on Guatemala in number, openly this time. The rationale for the coup had been that Guatemala was a 'bridgehead for Communism'. Now the evidence of Russian involvement could be uncovered. Many thousands of documents had fallen into the CIA's hands. Its operatives would unearth the secret links and reveal, as it were, where the bodies were buried. Here was the agency's chance to expose Soviet intentions to turn Guatemala into a military base. The CIA set about searching through the documents.

As time dragged on, nothing substantial emerged. There was some indication that Moscow had attempted to build a bridgehead into the minds of the nation's young. The Russians had sent teaching materials like schoolbooks. Even some of the most pliant journalists covering the story shook their heads and ignored such evidence in their reports or suggested it might have been planted. Mrs María Arbenz's well stocked library attracted a good deal of attention. There was a biography of Stalin and works on Mao Tse-Tung's agrarian reform in China. The CIA kept hunting, looking for the signs of nascent hemispheric conspiracy: transfers of funds, networks of couriers and correspondence with Moscow.

Finally some evidence was discovered of clearly sympathetic communication between Guatemala and the Kremlin. The Russians had written requesting a shipload of bananas. The Guatemalans wrote back saying sorry, that United Fruit ran the banana business and the government had no powers to get the fruit to Russia. Guatemala evidently toed United Fruit's line, not Moscow's.

United Fruit had experienced tremors in the past but the real earthquake came as the Department of Justice was allowed to go ahead with its case against the company. Previously United Fruit had avoided such assaults one way or another, by being out of sight and mind or beyond jurisdiction, by political manoeuvering or string pulling, or by stamping its feet. For the first time, the company was unable to get its own way. The Justice Department had always been called off in the past and this time someone had waved it through.

John Foster Dulles greatly regretted the judicial move. It was against all his instincts but, after consideration, he had reluctantly agreed to it. United Fruit had gone too far. It was not any company deed in particular, more the context of the desperate times. There were too many Castros and others as yet undiscovered, like Guevara, using United Fruit to justify their cause. The US had observed the widespread protests across Latin America after the Guatemalan coup. Though most of those taking part in such demonstrations might be gullible and misled, it would still be necessary to educate them and lead them along the right path. This would be easier if United Fruit, in its manifestation as 'octopus', was not blocking the way.

The extent of this 'betrayal' was staggering to United Fruit. A crusader in the Western cause, it was being treated as little better than a Communist, and possibly worse. The implication was that it was a traitor and was losing America the Cold War. The company's problem was, however, similar to those it had suffered in the past. United Fruit had often strayed across the line between what was officially regarded as right and wrong. Generally it had managed to retreat in time and to rejoin those who controlled society's 'unseen mechanism', as Edward Bernays, the company's venerable propaganda adviser, had put it. United Fruit was being characterised again as a 'nasty trust', though not because anyone on high had suddenly discovered it had been mistreating the poor and dispossessed. It had wandered out of the realm of normal business, where it could get away with an awful lot, into an area where its actions were more likely to be noticed and cause offence to those who could retaliate.

The company had previously angered the two presidents Roosevelt over its interference in 'strategic' matters. In Teddy's time, in the first decade of the twentieth century, United Fruit stood in the way of his hiring the Jamaican labour he wanted to build the Panama Canal and had to take action to divert the attentions of the president's anti-trust people. It had sold several companies, in which it had bought a controlling interest, back to the original owners, including Sam 'Banana Man' Zemurray. Another company was that owned by some Italian families and which, though only small, had been named Standard Fruit. Thirty years later, the Second World War had diverted President Franklin D. Roosevelt from having his anti-trust lawyers act against the company after it had been so keen on trade with Nazi Germany. Now President Eisenhower's administration had returned to focusing on United Fruit's activities for fear it was inciting revolution.

Edward Bernays knew precisely what to do and reached for his dog-eared contact list. He made a few calls to old friends who responded with a number of newspaper articles suggesting a coincidence between what Communists had failed to do in Guatemala and what Washington was doing now. In the best style of Senator Joseph McCarthy, the articles implied that Communists remained in deeper recesses of government and were still intent on bringing down such a national institution as United Fruit.

Enthused by its earlier move into film-making with *Journey to Banana Land*, United Fruit produced another contribution to the genre. This twelve-and-a-half-minute film quickly came to the point that United Fruit was fighting for the West and liberty. The company propaganda department gave much attention to the film and carefully chose its title of *Why the Kremlin*

Hates Bananas. Its title frame showed three bananas arriving like tourists at the walls of the Kremlin, whose cupolas were transformed into the anguished faces of the Soviet Cabinet, or Politburo. It was imaginative and for a while held in high esteem within the company, if not high enough to be released to the outside world. United Fruit itself soon sensed it was embarrassing and eventually, in Kremlin-like mode, would destroy the prints.

The hopes of Bernays and the company had been stymied by Senator McCarthy's public fall from grace. Ironically, the success of United Fruit in having the Guatemalan government overthrown played its part. Shortly before the coup, McCarthy had accused Allen Dulles's CIA of being infiltrated by Communists, whereupon the agency had immediately been able to show that any accusations McCarthy had made against it and the Eisenhower administration must have been absurd. The senator trailed away to continue ruining his liver, died three years later and is usually remembered in the US as an isolated moment in history when the country went a little haywire.

In arguing its case against the Department of 'Injustice', as the company called it, United Fruit was somewhat restrained by the fact that there were people in high government positions who knew its business as well as the company did. The Dulles brothers had advised it in days when it had been quietly increasing its monopoly hold on Guatemala through control of the railroad. The company continued to dispute the anti-trust case for several years but mainly ran up against Washington's wish to be seen behaving in a different way in Latin America, with Guatemala as an example.

The US plan was both to ditch Arbenz's land reform and

ditch United Fruit's monopoly. Washington's rationale appeared to be that Guatemala's multitude of peasant farmers, contrary to what they certainly believed, didn't need more land. They needed more capitalism. United Fruit's Guatemalan assets were, therefore, to be broken up, albeit quite gradually, and distributed among its competitors. Quite a lot of them went to the Standard Fruit Company, United Fruit's one-time insignificant rival, among others in the international banana trade.

In Costa Rica, United Fruit's oldest country of operation, its leader Pepe Figueres had other ideas. Figueres had previously decided that the best way to keep his army out of politics was to abolish it and turn its quarters into an art gallery. Next he planned to do some wider remodelling of Costa Rican society. Figueres had been educated at one of the US's, and Boston's, finest institutions, the Massachusetts Institute of Technology, and he had a Swedish wife. His plan for Costa Rica reflected a mix of these influences; he proudly pronounced that he was a capitalist and a Social Democrat. Costa Rica needed more schools, hospitals and other demonstrations of a welfare state, he said. It would be extremely rare for Latin America, he added, but fortunately Costa Rica had the means to pay for it. For this, he looked to United Fruit, a loyal friend and an integral member of Costa Rican society for some eighty years. He ordered the company to cough up 60 per cent of its profits.

Figueres got away with it. Hereafter, with its elected government, a European-style welfare system and relatively ordered life on its mesa, the country's high central plateau, Costa Rica called itself the 'Switzerland of Central America'. When Figueres devised his scheme, the company was not in a position to oppose it. It had the US Justice Department to fight and anyway, so soon after Guatemala wasn't the best time for another coup. The US government came to the same conclusion. Vice-president Richard Nixon was sent down to check on this character and his country. Figueres and his wife entertained Nixon and his wife on a United Fruit plantation. The natives around them were apparently happy. A smiling Figueres fed his guests company bananas. Nixon munched his dourly, kept his shirt cuffs buttoned in the humidity and couldn't quite put his finger on the problem. Then he went away.

Far bigger troubles were emerging. United Fruit's manipulation of the press during the Guatemalan operation had prompted a reaction among the Fourth Estate. Journalists reflected, didn't like what had been done to them and resolved 'never again'. Several went to Cuba to look for Fidel Castro and his forces now ensconced somewhere in the Sierra Maestra in the south-east of the island. One of them, Herbert Matthews, managed to get through to Castro at his camp. Castro kept Matthews confined to the camp, for the journalist's 'own safety' in this dangerous habitat where the troops of President Fulgencio Batista's government were attempting to hunt Castro down. Castro had his own men roam at distance from the camp, firing randomly to give the impression there were far more of them than there were. In his dispatches, Matthews expressed himself impressed by Castro's character and resolve. Previous reports, emanating from the Cuban regime and its supporters in the US government, had said that Castro's forces were nothing more than a few bandits in the hills.

Castro was a son of United Fruit. The company had financed his upbringing and education as well as that of his brother

Raúl. Their father was a relatively wealthy Cuban who had leased land from United Fruit and sold the sugar he grew to the company. Fidel Castro spoke some English, was Jesuit-educated and mixed with company people at garden parties and other social occasions. Years later old United Fruit men would reminisce and wonder how it had all gone so wrong. Fidel and Raúl had been such good lads.

Castro walked into Havana and into power on New Year's Day 1959. The regime of Batista and its support from the US fell away. Castro was acclaimed in the streets and, for a while, also enjoyed favourable US opinion. He gave a major speech at Guantánamo, pointedly near to the US base that had maintained its presence on the island. Castro spoke of Cuba's past, present and future without exciting great alarm in the US, though some sober mention was made in the press of what he had to say about the United Fruit Company. He had called it a 'grave social problem'.

United Fruit was involved in a betrayal of its own. It was trying to dump the banana. The fruit was far less profitable than it had been due to disease-related expense. Ever more land clearances and chemical treatments meant bananas cost $2,500 an acre to produce, five times more than they had in the 1930s. Experts in the field spoke of a 'reversal in banana economics'. Once upon a time, costs had been stable and markets expanding; now markets were static and costs exploding.

Big Mike was exploding too. Pumped full of fertilisers to add weight and profit, it was today more like 'Fat Mike'. Fertilisers also caused banana plants to grow taller and more vulnerable to hurricanes. 'Thus acts of God have not been wholly unsolicited,' wrote one journalistic sceptic. In 1958 a hurricane in Guatemala blew down 80 per cent of the Tiquisate plantation.

United Fruit moved on manfully, seeking to abandon the long-standing partner that had lost its looks. 'Diversification' was the new keynote of business and chief executives fancied themselves as Renaissance men, not one-trick dullards. A company producing one item may have been a mark of solidity in the past but modern corporations spread the load, cut the risk and mastered varied portfolios. United Fruit wanted to become a 'conglomerate' like others that were so much a part of the scene and venture into profitable fields. It prospected for oil and metals, entirely new experiences for an old plantation company. Clearly cursed with bad luck, it failed to strike it rich.

Its managers claimed that the company's problem was that it should have diversified earlier. The end of the Second World War would have been the time for a change of plan and for United Fruit to build anew. At that stage, however, so many people had been in thrall to Carmen Miranda, the 'Good Neighbor' from the south, with her provocative eyes, dance rhythms and songs that captivated her audience. Miranda did not make a penny out of it and had died aged forty-six in 1955. For her pains, she had been criticised at home for allowing herself and Latin America to be patronised. United Fruit had made millions out of Señorita Chiquita Banana but now found it was too late to adapt.

The company could not offload its old sidekick and tried a familiar reconciliation. It would try to change and remould the banana into something more excitingly diverse. Dessicated banana chips and banana essence for ice cream became the next big items on the agenda and quite failed to spark interest in the marketplace.

United Fruit's board did not know where to turn next. It was in the hands of some of the best and oldest families of Boston. A Jefferson Coolidge had lately retired as chairman and been succeeded by a Peabody Gardner. No bunch of bananas was better connected. As to the future, what were United Fruit's plans in the face of disease and such severe disappointments?

Someone asked Al Bump, head honcho during the hard times in Guatemala and now back in Boston as vice-president for tropical operations. An engineer with twenty years in the field, he would know: 'Grow more bananas,' said Bump.

'Something' had to be done about Cuba, and that something was to be an act of historical infamy. United Fruit's cane fields there had gone up in flames. Its properties had been seized, its plantation managers beaten and chased away, even murdered. The government of Fidel Castro regarded United Fruit as one of the companies that had represented *yanqui* imperialism for as long as most people could remember. United Fruit regarded itself as the respectable face of US business on the island.

A whole historic industry disappeared in smoke. The company had its large sugar estates in the north-east of the island around such towns as Preston and Banes. Minor Keith had built a throbbing infrastructure of railway lines serving the plantations. In United Fruit's heyday, locomotives from the great age of steam had burst from their sheds with broad, bowed cowcatchers up front. They ran through United Fruit's expansive pastures where thousands of head of cattle grazed. Yet the company had always maintained an aloofness from Cuban life.

Fidel Castro had put things more starkly when, at Guantánamo, he had spoken of United Fruit as a grave social problem. The company grew huge amounts of sugar but neglected to buy very much from the island's producers. Many were small farmers who could have used the patronage. Castro's father had been one of the lucky ones. United Fruit had also failed to realise the potential of the business, or if it had, the company had done little about it. The residue of sugar cane was the fibrous mass known as bagasse. One day Brazil would run cars on it and, although no one knew about that yet, bagasse was known to convert quite easily into saleable newsprint and wallboard. Mixed with molasses, bagasse also acted as a binder for cattle food. Molasses was a by-product of sugar and United Fruit had to feed its herds of cattle. It had failed to make the connection, while half a dozen Cuban companies with far more limited resources were building bagasse-processing plants on the island.

Castro and his national bank president, Che Guevara, knew about United Fruit's penchant for accounting fiddles. The company routinely undervalued its profits, which were just shipped abroad and away. Thomas McCann, formerly of United Fruit's PR department, in recording his thoughts about life in Cuba noted that the company contrived to have very little money left each year for investment in the island. It was hardly enough 'to float the Cuban manager's yacht'.

Fidel Castro may have been a son of the local bourgeoisie but he wasn't much of a man for yachts. He was a martinet, who had done away with the brothels and the sex shows and the casinos in Cuba run by Meyer Lansky and his generic business friends in 'the Mob'. United Fruit was not so damaged by this crackdown on the island's leisure and entertainment sector, since it had stopped its cruises on the Great White Fleet a couple of years before. Other, and specialist, cruise lines proliferated and people were less inclined anymore to travel second-class to a banana. In Cuba, nonetheless, the company estimated its losses as a result of the revolution at $60 million.

The state of the company's fortunes remained under sympathetic observation by Howard Hunt. The CIA had seen Operation Success work well in Guatemala in 1954 and felt it could be put into action again in Cuba. It would be dusted off for reuse and renamed. 'Operation Zapata' struck the right optimistic note. It was audacious enough to announce where the invasion of Cuba was to be, which was the Zapata peninsula in the south-west of the island at the Bay of Pigs.

Hunt's CIA boss, Allen Dulles, was perfectly happy with the idea. President Eisenhower was far more worried about the prospects for intervention in Cuba. He gave his approval because his field commanders said such action was necessary yet he agonised that it could be 'our Black Hole of Calcutta'. This was effectively no longer his watch, however, since Ike had nearly served two presidential terms. Vice-president Richard Nixon, on the other hand, dreamed that the chances of his landing the presidency at the 1960 elections would be much assisted by Cuba returning to the fold as Americans went to cast their votes. Conceivably, Nixon imagined one of the Great White Fleet making a triumphant return to Havana harbour with him waving from the rail. Even if that would have been a little too fanciful, United Fruit did make two of its boats available for the imminent Cuban exercise.

In the US, the mission had succeeded before it started. Cubans who had fled the island run by Castro swaggered around Miami with chequebooks and promises of how easy it would soon be to go back and throw him out. They imagined a re-run of the Guatemalan invasion, with the arrival of a 'liberation force' of exiles and the crowds cheering in the streets. Castro was a tyrant and he would just have to be toppled for the Cuban people to rise up in joy and relief.

Guatemala was logically chosen as a launch pad but illogically failed to meet expectations. Although the army had accepted United Fruit's coup of 1954, many junior officers objected to the use of their territory for an attack on another country. Guatemala was being used like a banana republic, they complained. In Nicaragua, the Somoza family remained ever faithful. They put Puerto Cabezas and other areas of the Mosquito Coast at the disposal of the CIA for training and the launching of air strikes.

The planning fell behind and during the US election campaign there was no sign of the operation's launch. John F. Kennedy, the Democratic candidate, taunted Nixon, saying the Republicans talked a big game in the Cold War about Berlin and other remote locations while they did nothing about Castro's Cuba, which was ninety miles away and nine minutes by jet. Nixon was frustrated because, like many people, he knew of the plan to overthrow Castro but could not talk about what remained an official secret. The delays continued until after the election when Kennedy, not Nixon, was in the White House.

The new president could hardly call off the operation, having himself urged that action be taken. In April 1961, two ships lent by United Fruit's Great White Fleet were among the seven that sailed to the Bay of Pigs. The boats almost steamed right onto the reefs that no one seemed to have realised were there.

The invasion force of exiled Cubans soon did, as, under fire, they waded across the coral, feet unprotected, boots around their necks, rifles raised above the waves. Those who weren't shot in the surf were shot on the beaches or captured and laid face down on the sand. Members of Castro's defence force ran across some of them dragging chainsaws. No towns spontaneously rose in support of the exiles. Some survivors made it back, swimming through the shark-infested waters to the boats off shore. Operation Zapata was an abject failure.

11
Decline and Fall

The Kennedy administration blamed the CIA for the Bay of Pigs debacle and Allen Dulles, its director, resigned for this 'failure of intelligence'. Those who had lost their assets in Cuba since Fidel Castro's takeover blamed President John F. Kennedy for not allowing a sufficient number of air strikes to support the invasion. The two sides to the debate evaded the point of whether the invasion should have ever taken place and whether it had been far more characteristic of a bygone world.

Sam Zemurray died, aged eighty-four, in November 1961, in retirement in Louisiana. Fifty years earlier he had launched the invasion of Honduras and boasted a stunning success. As a result of this latest exercise in military intervention by United Fruit, the company had been humiliated.

That did not prevent the company still making an impact. The Guatemalan coup of 1954 had led to the Bay of Pigs invasion of 1961, as a result of which Fidel Castro invited, or allowed, the Soviet Union to place nuclear missiles on the island. This provoked the 1962 Cuban missile crisis, the Cold War incident thought to have been the nearest mankind has come to the end of the world. No one would have remotely imagined it had anything to do with bananas.

As for the assassination of President Kennedy in November 1963, the conspiracy theories have been many and varied. United Fruit, with its famously ubiquitous tentacles, might find its part in them. Boston's Wasps and its Catholic Kennedys had not always got along. Of those who had lost Cuban property, United Fruit had reason to feel as betrayed as any by Kennedy. Many of the stories of a plot to kill the president featured New Orleans, the company's old southern capital. Lee Harvey Oswald, the assassin-to-be, had an office in the city's International Trade Mart building as did William Gaudet, 'Bill', the magazine editor associated with Edward Bernays' early propaganda efforts for the company and friend of the CIA. Oswald and Gaudet appeared to have travelled to Mexico together. This was a short while before the assassination in Dallas, north across the Mexican–US border. Howard Hunt, asked in 2004 by *Slate.com* whether he had been in Dallas on the day, answered 'no comment'. Nothing can be construed, of course, and all such 'evidence' is at best circumstantial. It may only show how easy it is to construct the skeleton of a conspiracy theory.

The Gros Michel, Big Mike, had finally succumbed to disease. At great cost United Fruit tore down its plantations and planted a new banana throughout Central America. This was the Cavendish, whose origins lay in the soon-to-be-defoliated forests of Vietnam, or possibly India. England's Lord Cavendish had happened upon it in the days of the Raj, taken it back and nurtured it in the greenhouse of his stately home of Chatsworth in Derbyshire. The Cavendish wasn't as fat and long as the Big Mike and its key virtue in commercial terms was that it was said to be disease resistant. It was not United Fruit that delivered to market this new variety and potential saviour of the business. Its rival Standard Fruit had done most of the development work, implying United Fruit was not the power of old.

Belatedly United Fruit had started producing in Ecuador. Thomas Cabot had suggested the idea in the 1940s and had been sacked for his pains by Sam Zemurray. Cabot had also pointed out that the labour unions were not very strong in Ecuador. When United Fruit set up shop in the country, therefore, there was no pressure from the local workforce to build hospitals and schools. United Fruit had always built its hospitals and schools to make sure it could attract people from the US. Now it wondered whether it should bother.

This new 'Third World' in which many people were living had its attractions. The term had only recently been coined. The first world was the West and the second the East as run by the Soviet Union. The third was the impoverished remainder. The first and second sides in the equation vied over whether, respectively, the free market or social welfare should be paramount. Each tried to resist the other but the first world had absorbed some of the influences of welfare and the people of the second wanted more free market. In the Third World most people thought themselves lucky to have a job.

United Fruit also had the revelatory idea of giving people their own land. These were substantial pieces, whole plantations. The company had been under pressure to allow producers more independence for years but had not until now been struck by the advantages. If it turned over plantations to the locals, this would stop their complaining. They would be less inclined to accuse the company of being 'El Pulpo'. Also they would have to take responsibility for themselves, the diseases that afflicted the banana and the problems of running the business. It occurred to United Fruit that, for all these years and for all the criticism it had received about exploitation, it had been as much a welfare organisation as a proper business. It had taken care of people's bugs in its hospitals and, at vast expense, those of the banana in the company's purpose-built laboratories. Now it passed the affairs of the plantation over to the local people. It could as easily maintain control of them further along the business chain, in shipping and marketing. The new 'independent' producers still needed to get their bananas shipped and sold and wouldn't be able to do so without United Fruit.

There were, however, more disturbing hints here of the company not being what it had been. Of old New England Puritan stock, it was a firm believer in the work ethic. It was a company that had always engaged in production and that proudly got its 'hands dirty'. It was becoming more of a manipulator than a producer and losing its old self-esteem.

One independent producer it did not want around was Aristotle Onassis, the Greek shipping magnate, who in the early 1960s offered to buy United Fruit's Panamanian plantations. He was someone who as a producer could take care of himself and wouldn't need to be dependent on United Fruit. He may have wanted to buy the plantations to build a bridgehead in Panama in order to take over the Panama Canal. The US, the canal's owner, might just have agreed. The waterway was becoming obsolete for modern shipping and Onassis, with his billions, had the resources to upgrade the canal. Everyone would have been happy, except his rivals in business who would have had to pay extortionate rates to get their ships through the canal while his went free. It was an idea worthy of Minor Keith, United Fruit's old leader who had maintained such a grip on Central America's railways. United Fruit was alive to this and turned Onassis down.

The company still thought it had the powers to stay in front of the pack. It took an important step in 'branding', which was still not a generic term except in the world of cattle ranching. Brands such as Rolls-Royce, Hoover and Coca-Cola emerged by commercial osmosis. United Fruit's method was more akin to that of a cowhand with a hot iron aimed at the rump of a steer. It stuck small labels on its bananas with the image of Señorita Chiquita Banana. The company realised that for years she had gyrated for the benefit of all producers, as consumers who saw and liked her bought the first bananas they put their hands on. The new idea was to help them differentiate theirs from the rest. United Fruit had its labels put on every third banana, upwards of two billion stickers a year.

United Fruit was 'playing God' and laying claim to a thing of nature. That seemed appropriate enough, given that the company had created the modern banana. In reality, this form of branding was not entirely original. Californian fruit growers had shipped products with colourful labels since the 1880s. United Fruit had also adapted the idea from its long-term marriage with Fyffes, a case of something borrowed, something blue. Fyffes had introduced its blue label as long ago as 1929. Señorita Chiquita's image on their bananas provided an exciting new impetus to the as-yet-underdeveloped art of branding. It was more like alchemy than art. A label applied by a lowly paid worker many hundreds of miles away somehow represented a mark of quality in the marketplace and was at first a great success. Sales jumped and gave the company renewed edge over the competition, though briefly. There was nothing to stop rivals introducing their own labels, which they soon did.

United Fruit missed a great opening in the 1960s. The decade had started promisingly enough as Harry Belafonte, the US singer who had been brought up in Jamaica, had his big hit with 'The Banana Boat Song'. The Caribbean world that the calypso conjured was one with which United Fruit would have loved to have been associated, as tired yet contented workers sang after a full night humping stems into a ship's hold.

A little further into the 1960s, Belafonte had reassessed his earlier lyrics and had become a leading activist in the civil rights movement. He was a link to the white middle class and pulled its stars on board, the already established Pete Seeger and the emerging Bob Dylan and Joan Baez among them. Civil rights marches and demonstrations turned violent when attacked in such places as Selma, Alabama, the town where Sam Zemurray had settled after leaving the anti-Semitism of Russia.

Protests quickly acquired an added edge. At the time of the Guatemalan crisis in 1954, President Eisenhower had warned the French to back off from involvement in Central American diplomacy that was being acted out at the UN. He had said that if they didn't, then they could expect no US help in Vietnam. The same year, France had suffered the military defeat at Dien Bien Phu that led it to leave Vietnam. In place of the French, the CIA, emboldened by its success in Guatemala had stepped up clandestine involvement in Vietnam. By the mid-1960s it was the US that was embroiled.

Within the political turmoil and anti-war protests in the US at the time, a peculiar thing happened. United Fruit became fashionable. The most notorious of capitalist constructs acquired an edge of radical chic. The banana was the heart of it and crowds began to call out its name: 'Ba-na-na!' they chanted at a large rally (or Be-in), on Easter

Sunday, 1967 in New York's Central Park. In Bernays' day the company would have relished the PR. Members of the assembled mass in New York carried large banana effigies. What did this symbolise – peace, innocence, disrespect? The crowd looked the 'alternative' type, slovenly dressed and with many of its number in T-shirts. Worse, many of the T-shirts bore United Fruit's Señorita Chiquita logo. This was blatant theft of someone else's image. Furthermore it was being pilfered by these demonstrators for quite the wrong purposes. These people weren't United Fruit people but 'agitators'. President Richard Nixon would soon have another word for them. Nixon was to return from the political wilderness to win the presidency in 1968 and he called this class of person 'bums'.

United Fruit panicked when it discovered that dissidents were also using the banana for another inappropriate purpose: they were smoking it. 'Banana heads' were said to have discovered the fruit's gift for producing an hallucinogenic high. Bananas, that had once been pushed as an alternative for meat for the working classes, now were being promoted as a substance to relax the discontented children of the middle-class. The fruit was touted as a cheap and legal alternative to LSD.

When the company's distinguished forbears had driven prices down and created the mass market this was hardly what they would have imagined. Whether all this talk of highs was hokum or not, it swept across the market from coast to coast. The alternative press, which was becoming quite popular as well as mainstream, printed recipes for how to scrape, boil and bake your own. No recipe from United Fruit's home economics department had ever been like that. The result tasted like compost, some said, but proved far more successful than United

Fruit's former line in bananas and bacon. A 'banana-buying boom' registered from San Francisco to Boston, from Haight-Ashbury to Harvard Square.

The banana slipped into popular culture. There was Donovan singing 'Mellow Yellow'. Andy Warhol produced his album cover for The Velvet Underground and Nico portraying a banana with a zip that you could pull back. This was considered very good fun for the modern breed, though any oldsters that might have been tempted to take a closer look would have been in for a surprise. Pulling back the zip did not reveal an innocently pale piece of fruit but something pink. From United Fruit's perspective the type of people who played this kind of prank were disgusting.

United Fruit didn't get the joke and missed the moment. It countered all allegations that it was allied to the cause of 'peace and love' with dull detail. It cited reports from the government and the nation's best universities in defence of its case that the banana had no dangerous neuro-chemical qualities. Failing to embrace the time, in the counter-culture the company saw only the wrong people when, in fact, they were fast turning into the right people: articulate, intelligent and with prospects. Theirs was becoming the established way of thinking and the view that demanded to be listened to. As these new thinkers moved towards joining those controlling the inner mechanism, United Fruit was being pushed to the margins.

The members of the United Fruit board met Eli Black on their territory. They repaired to the Algonquin Club on Boston's Commonwealth Avenue. It was among the brownstone town houses in the Back Bay adjacent to the Charles River. The building stood out with its flat grey masonry, managing to be a 'cut above' and solidly conservative. In the library, with its dark panelled ceilings and graveside sobriety, hung portraits of old club presidents.

The Wasps suspected they knew what Black would be like: he'd be hyperactive New York, probably loud and a 'can-do' man looking to muscle in on a world accustomed to the gentle passage of ships. He had called up that morning to announce himself as the mystery buyer of a large block of shares they had been worrying about for the past few days. He would fly up to Boston that afternoon.

Black was not fazed by his surroundings and, like his hosts, was understatedly polite. He understood that United Fruit was a proud company fiercely protective of its tradition. Would he uphold its values in the future? After dinner the board still worried that he wouldn't.

United Fruit looked for other suitors among those it trusted. It thought it had found one in Textron, an established New England conglomerate. The parties reached the point of discussing possible names. United Fruit paid good money to one of the modern PR operations that were springing up everywhere and trading in matters of corporate image. Its representatives came up with several titles for the proposed new company, such as Panomega, Metromega and Corporad, none of which quite fitted the bill. The deal itself came to nothing. Other potential partners also made their excuses. The more some of them delved into the banana business the more they learned about its diseases and associated costs. It had all looked very straightforward at first. 'What's the big deal?' said one would-be suitor. 'So you have dinner once a year with the president of Honduras.' Finally Black was the only one in the race.

Black had retired into the background at this point. Ever the salesman, he had made his pitch and it was time to shut up and let the other side agonise over how to respond. Amid the market speculation about his bid, the price of the shares he had bought went up and up. He would make money even if United Fruit turned him down, although as time passed it became clear it would not. Wall Street relished the thought of Black breathing new life into old United Fruit. He was a thrusting 'asset manager' who would take hold of a company that for years had mismanaged its assets. Black would sort things out. As one expert said, 'whether he knows a banana plant from a potted palm is largely irrelevant'. Amid the excitement, Wall Street brushed aside rumours that there had been something remiss about Black's mass purchase of the company's shares.

The financial community backed the idea of the company entering the modern age, some reminiscing about the 'nasty' United Fruit of old. Slave traders and exploiters had founded it when, after the Civil War, looking for other outlets for their dubious talents they had happened upon bananas. The pioneers of the business had been no better than 'conquistadors' and among the 'wildest and greediest men in history', said New York's *Fortune* magazine. Their list of sins 'would hold even the prurient eye of a browser in a Times Square bookstore'. Lately, however, United Fruit had transformed itself into a distinguished giant, the largest employer in Central America and the one that built hospitals and schools for its people.

One worry that received attention was that, not so far back in United Fruit's past, it had appeared in court. It had had that bitter anti-trust row over its affairs in Guatemala, as a result of which lands had been redistributed among its rivals and its monopoly over Minor Keith's railroad taken away. The problem with this was that United Fruit's name was 'on file'. Any further difficulties, and that file would likely be re-opened. It was the way of law enforcement agencies to haul in the usual suspects and United Fruit would be an especially good one for them. It was old and tired and had plenty in its past for the regulators, the hyenas of the jungle, to return to and scavenge. The politicians, press and public would not care if the real offenders escaped, just as long as someone, or something, was brought to book. Then everyone would forget about it: case closed.

Under Eli Black's leadership, United Fruit appeared to get off to a good start. As a sideline to its operations in Central America, the company had business interests in the US, in California for example, growing other agricultural products like lettuce. César Chávez, the union leader of the Mexicans who worked the fields, demanded new contracts for this underpaid and generally much abused labour force. Black said he would agree to the contracts, much to the surprise of his own management and to the chagrin of other big companies in the mucky world of agribusiness. More appreciative and no less amazed observers wondered whether they were witnessing a new enlightened United Fruit.

The company still had some of its more traditional touch. In 1969 the so-called 'Football War' broke out between Honduras and El Salvador. The two countries had long-standing frontier disputes that erupted after an especially fiery soccer game. El Salvador invaded United Fruit's old ally Honduras, in the process taking the trouble to seize some radio installations the company used to supervise its Pacific shipping. The Salvadorean government made fleeting propaganda from its confronting the imperial majesty of United Fruit. In response, the company made a few calls on behalf of itself and Honduras and before long the Organisation of American States had arranged a truce. With Black, it seemed, some of the former glory might have returned.

Black saw himself as a scholar, an intellectual and a man of books. He took some pride in his library. It was, however, doubtful that he was much of a reader since chief executives normally had little time for such activities. In 1970, he may have missed, therefore, the publication, in translation, of Gabriel García Márquez's *One Hundred Years of Solitude*. What overtook United Fruit next, as it moved towards its last years and days, might have come from the pages of the book, with its pestilence, war and biblical winds.

It began with an earthquake. In the middle of the night, two days before Christmas in 1972, Managua, the capital of Nicaragua, was destroyed. The earthquake ruined all but a handful of the buildings in the centre of the city, including the cathedral. Black quickly spotted the disaster's potential for United Fruit. He might not have known that he was continuing in the tradition of the company's philanthropy, but saw that food, shelter, water, medicines and the general basics of life were urgently needed. Black instructed civil engineers from United Fruit's other Central American areas to go to the disaster area straightaway. Advertisments appeared in US newspapers and on radio and television networks appealing for funds for the Nicaraguan Earthquake Emergency Drive, NEED. The advertisements identified NEED's munificent corporate sponsor.

United Fruit revived its skills as a film-maker, somewhat neglected since *Why the Kremlin Hates Bananas*. The company crafted a short movie starring Eli Black portraying United Fruit's relief efforts in Managua. The Nicaraguan disaster and the company's response to it were central features of United Fruit's next annual report. The company had done good works and should be proud to say so. It was an example to other big companies that, if they only made the effort, they could break out of the constricting confines of the narrow commercial world. United Fruit trumpeted 'Our Social Responsibility'.

Soon the chain of events began that led to Black's suicide. 1973 sounded the death knell for United Fruit as the ominously named black sigatoka hit plantations. This new variant of banana disease had no known antidote. In the same year company morale plunged when, for the first time, its banana sales fell behind that of another company, Standard Fruit, the corporation later better known as the sonorous Dole.

The Middle East war in the autumn of 1973 prompted OPEC to raise oil prices sharply and the banana-producing countries to set up their own cartel, UPEB. As Central America set about exacting revenge on United Fruit for the abuses of history, the forces of nature rejoined the battle the following spring when Hurricane Fifi devastated Honduras's plantations. With Black's fortunes failing, Wall Street returned to the question of his share deals at the time of his takeover of the company, suggesting that illicit trading had been involved. Word circulated that journalists had got hold of the story of his bribes to the Honduran military junta. Black faced disgrace both for his business failure and for what would be labelled his outrageous effort to sort it out.

Looking through the glass of his office window at a dull winter's dawn, Black smashed into it with his leaden briefcase.

He had filled it with books from his library. He threw the briefcase out, climbed onto the window ledge and jumped. United Fruit's world, its century of conspiracies and plans, therefore, came down to the final act of one deranged man.

12
Old and Dark Forces

The tumultuous events of the first half of the 1970s left the West and capitalism in need of redemption. What went on and who was involved could not be easily dismissed as the affairs of loveable rogues. An alliance of corrupt government and big companies was a familiar tale in Central America but not in the large and powerful countries that fought in freedom's name. It had turned into what looked like a 'United Fruit' world out there and it was United Fruit itself that was going to have to go.

What became known as the Watergate scandal began in mid-1972 and led to President Richard Nixon's exit from grace two years later. It entailed a story of intrigue that would have done United Fruit proud and out of it, once again, emerged Howard Hunt, the company's old CIA comrade.

Hunt had done well for the company in 1954 in Guatemala and not at all so well in 1961 at the Bay of Pigs in Cuba. Out of that crisis, he inherited the loyalty of a number of Cuban exiles that were fugitives from the regime of Fidel Castro. They needed work and took whatever Hunt gave them in the enduring fight against Communism. He had them break into Washington's Watergate Hotel, suites of which were being used as the Democratic Party's headquarters for the forthcoming elections. Nixon, the Republican incumbent was hotly favoured to win but people working on his behalf wanted to increase his chances by listening in to the Democrats' business. The Cubans were caught red-handed and, in a sense, redheaded, too. A red wig was found among the burglars' kit, which no one made any sense of at the time. The Cubans went to jail saying they had concocted the robbery alone and for their own reasons of 'anti-Communism'. They kept quiet otherwise, a service for which Hunt had promised them payment. He would also end up behind bars.

The investigation eventually led to Nixon, who had not known initially of the burglary but, when he did find out, had tried to cover up his staff's involvement. The president's nemesis was the US press, in particular Bob Woodward and Carl Bernstein, reporters employed by the *Washington Post*, who led a formidable campaign to hunt down the story. At the same time, it was the culmination of a process set in motion eighteen years before by United Fruit. While the company's assiduous efforts to manipulate the press at the time of the Guatemalan crisis in 1954 had paid off, they later had had strong repercussions, with a subsequent generation of journalists disinclined to believe anything that smacked of an official line. Favourable US press comment had helped Fidel Castro shed his image as a simple hill bandit and take power in 1959. Now over a decade on, the media had become highly critical of the US's war in Vietnam, and if there was anyone they were inclined to be sceptical about it was the man directing it, Richard Nixon, 'Tricky Dick'. The president hailed from the days of deception when a cowed press wrote what it was told. Nixon had made his reputation in the period following the Second World War as one of a small cabal hunting Communists in places that most people hadn't imagined they could possibly be. In the times of 1970s' dissent against the Vietnam War, the Watergate burglary implied a return to the old paranoia and that Nixon's Republican party had spied 'agitators' again in the Democratic party. In a televised address to the nation, Nixon claimed, 'I am not a crook.' The press proceeded to prove that in many people's minds he was and he resigned in August 1974.

It was through the good offices of the International Telephone & Telegraph Corporation (ITT) that certain ways of Central America had by this time introduced themselves to Chile. Hundreds of miles away in South America, the country had not been part of United Fruit's world; Chilean society prided itself on not being 'tropical', which meant corrupt and chaotic. Chile had a temperate, rather Mediterranean climate in most parts and a healthy democratic tradition, until it suddenly succumbed in the manner of a banana republic. General Pinochet strode in to overthrow the government of Salvador Allende, who had been elected in 1970. Thousands were killed and imprisoned in defence of freedom and Christian values, so Pinochet announced. Many people assumed the CIA's involvement and then it materialised that ITT was part of the story, too.

ITT had been more successful at being a conglomerate than United Fruit. As well as its large stake in Chile's national telephone company, it had international hotel, airline and car rental businesses. ITT's boss, Howard Geneen, or Hal to his friends, had been in league with the CIA in vain efforts to stop Allende winning the 1970 elections. Geneen was an accountant and the picture emerged after later hearings in the US Senate of him poring over his books decrying what he reckoned to be Chile's fall into chaos and the red. He and the CIA had

Pinochet seize power to restore their collective idea of order and balance.

ITT had also made another appearance, in the Watergate scandal and in a joint role with Howard Hunt in the case of Dita Beard and the 'man in the red wig'. Beard was a well-connected Washington lobbyist working for ITT. During the Watergate investigations, she had made a written statement that ITT had donated four hundred thousand dollars to President Nixon's Republican party. Beard had stated, it seemed, that the money was a bribe to have some anti-trust charges against ITT dropped. When reports of the statement came out Beard was taken ill and disappeared from view. Close family members thought only they knew where she was until, when her brother visited her in hospital, he found another man at her bedside. Or, he assumed it was a man, wearing badly applied women's make-up and a lop-sided red wig. Dita Beard soon withdrew her damaging statement about ITT payments to the Republican party, claiming that it was a gross forgery. The character who had hastened to her bedside was Hunt. The red wig was later apprehended with the Cuban burglars at the Watergate hotel.

If such cumulative sagas were any indication, government had lost all credibility and big business threatened to run out of control. All it needed for mankind's return to the jungle was for the robber barons to displace civil authority altogether. After all, they had tried in the past, as in the case of the moguls against President Roosevelt in the 1930s. Even as long ago as the Crash of 1873, others of their kind had said that the US was 'too democratic'. Now, a century later, the Middle East war had happened and illustrated that, while nation states and their peoples wilted under the strain, the big 'trusts' still came out of things very well.

Following the war in October 1973, big business's reputation plunged in more or less inverse proportion to the huge increases in oil company profits. The oil companies said it was not their fault because the OPEC cartel of oil-producing countries had raised the prices and the oil companies had only been unwitting beneficiaries. These protestations won few friends and sounded like the familiarly righteous line that the rich were condemned to prosper and the meek blessed in their suffering.

In fact, the oil prices hit rich and poor alike. In the US, whose dependence on the automobile traced back to Henry Ford's 'revolutionary' line in mass-produced Model Ts, the population was unable to go about its daily business. In the Third World, countries that were already impoverished found themselves pushed nearer to ruin. In the Social Democracies of Western Europe, experts spoke grimly of the 'death of the welfare state'. Once the higher price of oil had taken its toll on budgets, they said, there would be nothing left for the schools, hospitals and other services provided by governments and on which people had come to depend. Capitalism was a miserable and brutal thing.

In its vanguard, the major oil companies were untouchable. Too strong to be subjected to anything but a lot of abuse, they withstood it and began their efforts to turn matters around. It was good in these times of uncertainty, intoned their supporters, that some of our finest institutions were in such a rude state of health. The banks enjoyed similar fitness levels with profits doing very well thanks to a lot of recycled oil money from the Arab members of OPEC and others like the Shah of Iran. The dwindling legions of laissez-faire argued that this meant things were as they should be. Formerly primitive nations, in the mediaeval kingdoms of the desert, were being assisted in their rise to prosperity and development. Few who heard such pleas found them convincing.

Someone, or something, was going to have to suffer and United Fruit was in no position to defend itself. In the face of oil price rises and UPEB's threats no one was going to wage war again on the company's behalf, in fact quite the reverse.

To some extent United Fruit brought it upon itself. Here was the pay-off for the impressions, half-truths and lies traded as news in Guatemala twenty years before and that now had journalists hot on the trail for the deeper story behind any news lead. In the wake of Woodward and Bernstein, every journalist wanted their 'Watergate' scoop and every regulator, official or any other person in authority was only too anxious to display their probity.

United Fruit was weak and no longer a member of the invisible government that made the decisions as 'the true ruling power'. It was far more likely to be subjected to decisions taken on its behalf. After Black died and was found to have dined too lavishly with the president of Honduras, there was the added attraction that what it lacked in its old powers, United Fruit still evoked in potent memories. It could be sacrificed with impunity and make an impact at the same time. To be done with it would show how the business world, for all the questions raised, was quite capable of doing the moral and decent thing.

There was no conspiracy and the mystical way things had of working themselves out made United Fruit's demise look like natural selection. The stock market offloaded its shares and brought the company's market price crashing. The regulators moved in to seize its books and bring it to court. United Fruit was hustled off the street like a victim of the Central American death squads its activities had done much to encourage.

President Anastasio Somoza sat in his bunker unable to understand. He and his family had been the company's oldest friends and for generations had fought the good fight. They and their army had kept Nicaragua and the heart of Central America safe since the US marines had pulled out in the 1930s. Yet here they were being sold out to the Communists.

It was 1979 and Somoza had built the bunker after the Managua earthquake seven years before. The militarised compound was a line of squat bomb-proof structures next to the InterContinental Hotel, which was virtually the only building to have survived the disaster. He had expanded his business interests into construction, banking and anything through which earthquake relief funds could pass. At the same time, he had withdrawn into the bunker and himself. Managua remained a city only in name, its corpse lost beneath the tall grass beyond his door. Little reconstruction of any note had been carried out in the city centre and few people were left whom he could trust, as an alliance had built against him ranging from armed guerrillas to the disenchanted rich.

The president sat at the end of the long dark polished table in the bunker's Cabinet room, behind him on the wall a kind of patchwork quilt of the Nicaraguan eagle. On closer inspection, it was clear that some people previously seated at the table had spent time scratching their initials and other doodles. How they had managed this under the eye of the president might have been explained by his tendency to be transported away by the sound of his own voice.

Somoza's story was familiar: a few bandits assailed him from distant mountain hideaways. Radical priests had joined in and were sadly deluded people who should not concern themselves with politics. What they failed to grasp, Somoza went on, was that he had pitched himself against the greedy rich on behalf of the poor. As for Jimmy Carter, the US's present leader, Somoza found himself hard pushed to remain polite. Under Carter, the White House had taken leave of its senses and opened the way for Communism.

Actually, from what I understood, the guerrillas fighting Somoza were capable of seizing important towns just a couple of hours away north along the Pan-American Highway. As for radical members of the church, I had presumably travelled with two of them from Tegucigalpa in Honduras, elderly nuns from the US Midwest who had offered me a ride in their jeep. They had given up one version of Middle America for this one where their works among the poor were more greatly needed. Somoza's reference to the greedy rich may have been accurate with the proviso that their main gripe was that since the earthquake he had hogged all the best business opportunities. In the US, meanwhile, Carter's main foreign policy principle was human rights, which he had aimed at the Soviet Union first and then at such regimes as Somoza's.

In the old days, United Fruit could have made a few calls and help would have materialised. After the company's departure from Central America, along with its brand of US influence, other forces had filled the vacuum. Conventional wisdom had it that these were the extremes of left and right and certainly neither United Fruit nor the United States had done much in the past to nurture the forces of moderation. But the opposition to several of the present Central American governments went from the customary armed men and women in bandanas to the elderly and, hitherto, conservative Archbishop of San Salvador, Oscar Romero. Lately, the archbishop's sermons from the cathedral in El Salvador's capital had become more and more critical of his country's government and army.

Carter had become US president in 1977 proposing a form of New Deal for Latin America. He had signed treaties with Panama's leader, General Omar Torrijos, for the US to hand over control of the Panama Canal by the end of the century. Torrijos had taken a strident line on both the canal and United Fruit as symbols of *yanqui* imperialism in Latin America. The Panamanian leader had played a role in the death throes of the company by being the main organiser of the UPEB banana cartel and its efforts to extract more money out of the company.

When President Carter stopped military aid to some Central American regimes the bigger trouble started. Dissidence, street riots and guerrilla activity spread from Nicaragua across the region as opposition groups sought to rid themselves of their hard-line regimes. In El Salvador, the 'Fourteen Families' and their army came under sustained attack. Some towns of the Indian Highlands in Guatemala were under army occupation by day and that of guerrillas by night. Honduras remained relatively quiet, although an old United Fruit plantation I had visited was now being run as a workers'co-operative.

In Washington the talk was of the 'domino effect', a theme

that had much exercised strategic minds during the recent wars in South-East Asia, when Vietnam, Cambodia and Laos had in turn been drawn into war. Central America, however, wasn't some distant part of the world.

Somoza fell in July 1979 in Nicaragua, the guerrillas having made their way out of the mountains in force and to Managua along the Pan-American Highway. Somoza fled his bunker and the country and, thus, departed from power in the banana republic that grew few bananas. The new government set about a revolution to change the country's image to the accompanying din of alarm bells ringing in Washington.

Among Somoza's final words as he left for exile was that his fate had been sealed by 'Communist intervention'. It was a vague claim, aimed at anyone from Torrijos in Panama, who had unsettled matters in Latin America by wanting sovereignty over the Panama Canal, to China, who Somoza said had provided arms to his enemies. Although it was too late for him, like-thinking souls were listening.

Ronald Reagan came to the White House after the elections of 1980. His view was that Communists and agitators were again on the march and, though their causes varied, they were united in confirming that the US had lost its way.

Fundamentalist Muslims in Iran had forced the shah from power early in 1979. By the end of the year, the Soviet Union had grown sufficiently paranoid about fundamentalism in its own Muslim regions. Consequently, the Soviet Union had invaded and occupied its neighbour Afghanistan, on grounds that it was harbouring fanatics. Somoza's overthrow in Nicaragua fell neatly between the two events. As in Guatemala in 1954, Central America had presented itself both as a problem in its own right and as a potential solution to the wider question of how the US was to signal its return to being a power in the world.

For its treachery, Nicaragua had to be isolated and its revolution curbed. Reagan expressed this in his own folksy terms: Nicaragua must be forced to concede, he said, and 'say uncle'. A number of Catholic priests had taken posts in the Nicaraguan government. The Vatican, most notably Pope John Paul II, brought pressure to bear, insisting that they had no role to play in politics.

To Nicaragua's north, President Reagan increased military aid to address the plight of the Fourteen Families in El Salvador, which was in a state of war. Early in 1980 an army death squad had claimed the life of Archbishop Romero, who had been shot at his altar.

In Guatemala, the US was restricted to giving moral support to the regime. The Guatemalans would not accept other forms of aid because its military leaders since the 1954 coup had remained sensitive to the slurs that they were symbolic of a banana republic. The army, however, rampaged through the Indian Highlands, killing the population when it could not locate guerrillas, while the death squads concentrated on urban matters. When international protests were made, Reagan spoke up for Guatemala's leadership: it was taking a 'bum rap', he said, on human rights.

To Nicaragua's south, Costa Rica came under US pressure to play a bigger part in the region and even to set up a proper army again. The Costa Ricans rejected the idea and said they would stay neutral. Panama might have proved a more tricky case, its leader, Torrijos, no fan of anything that hinted of a United Fruit world. Whatever threat he posed disappeared in 1981 with his death in a timely plane crash.

President Reagan's opportunity for a show of direct US force came in 1983 in the Caribbean island of Grenada. In the southern Windward Islands, near Trinidad and the coast of Venezuela, Grenada had once been a United Fruit territory. It had not been so dependent on bananas as other company areas and, with a diversified agricultural economy, was a paradise by comparison. Lately its leader, Maurice Bishop, a left-wing nationalist, had been murdered after members of his Cabinet kicked him out of power claiming he was not left-wing enough. US airborne troops dropped in on Grenada to rectify the situation. This was not an invasion, as its PR officers pointed out, but a 'pre-dawn tactical insertion'. In fact it appeared to be a genuine liberation, as the Grenadian people greeted the US's arrival with cheers and jubilation on the streets.

In Central America one piece still needed to be manipulated into place for the job to be done. Honduras, Nicaragua's north-eastern neighbour, had to be involved. It had always been a tranquil backwater, Tegucigalpa, its capital without a railway, stranded high on the central plateau. Since Sam the Banana Man's invasion in 1911, Honduras had been United Fruit's most pliant ally. All that was needed was to find an ambassador who would see it as an exciting posting.

Appointed by the Reagan administration, ambassador John Negroponte arrived with an impressive record and a solid reputation for work. He had served in some tough posts in South-East Asia, which suggested he was not coming to Central America for a quiet time. He also answered his own phone. When I called it was US Thanksgiving, which I hadn't realised, and he was the only person except a marine guard working in the embassy that day. He invited me in for a chat, which turned into an hour of the ambassador taking the opportunity to address recent claims in the US press that he was turning Honduras into an 'armed camp'.

He insisted that there were no such plans. He was a professional diplomat and a family man, he pointed out, leaving me lost for the connection, though assuming he meant he was not the belligerent character portrayed in the press. It was an interesting interview, containing not much in the way of hard detail, but overall I took the ambassador on trust. Negroponte went on to a successful diplomatic career, the State Department even pulling him out of retirement two decades later at the time of the Iraq invasion to be the US ambassador to the UN. He proceeded to take charge of the occupied country for a while afterwards, before returning to Washington amid all the recriminations about undetectable 'Weapons of Mass Destruction'. He came back to investigate the Iraq invasion's 'failure of intelligence'. My failure at the time of the Central American intervention of 1983 had been that I had kept an open mind about his claim that Honduras would keep its air of tranquillity.

Areas of Honduras were turned into armed camps, notably those along the distant Mosquito Coast that had been prime locations for US adventure since the days of Minor Keith and Sam Zemurray and other much earlier pirates. Counter-revolutionary forces, the Contras, were armed and trained to take on Nicaragua's dissident government. The world learned of the exploits of Colonel Oliver North, the enterprising US officer assigned to organise the bizarre 'Iran-Contra' plan. The Reagan administration secretly agreed to sell arms to an apparently hostile regime in Iran, with Iran channelling its payments to the Contras. By such means the screw was turned on Nicaragua and, in the late 1980s, its revolution brought to its knees.

With its intervention in Central America, Washington not only defeated the threat posed by a small agricultural country seeking to cast off its status as a client state, but also sent its signals to the larger enemy that the US was back in its dominant role. The last battle of the Cold War had been fought on United Fruit's old Central American territory.

After the end of the Cold War, the banana-trading Wild Bunch prospered. As the Berlin Wall came down and East Berliners marched chanting and singing to Banana Land, the markets of Eastern Europe opened and for the first time in many years the world's leading banana companies invested in new plantations. Also, court cases against them rose. Workers covered in dust and spray from the mounting quantities of fertiliser and pesticide complained of ailments from fertility loss to cancer.

The companies strode forward regardless and their next move was to take legal action of their own in a landmark case. The world was the limit now that capitalism had won and could spread across the globe. The course of 'globalisation', a new term, was apparently set fair. Even the likes of Communist China and bureaucratic India would join in, urged on by their highly entrepreneurial diasporas. Elsewhere it was just a matter of removing a few barriers and to this end the Wild Bunch led the fight.

Back in the late 1970s, the case brought against United Fruit's owner, United Brands, over Eli Black's misdeeds had been quietly closed. A token fine of fifteen thousand dollars suggested that the offence was not as serious as it had originally been portrayed and was due recognition of the company's sacrificial services to the system. Its debt to society settled, a chastened, leaner United Brands eventually left town and changed its name. From the hothouse of New York it moved to the Midwest and Cincinnati, Ohio. Cincinnati was a quiet, hard-working town. Its German forefathers had turned away the railroad because, they pointed out, they already had canals. Chicago had taken the railway lines instead, leaving Cincinnati a little like Tegucigalpa in its way. It also had a touch of spice because for some reason, no one was quite sure why, Cincinnati cuisine specialised in chilli. With its renewed confidence and affluence at the end of the Cold War, United Brands restyled itself Chiquita, a name pleasantly resonant of the past.

In the mid-1990s Chiquita and the Wild Bunch lobbied Washington. Such skilled practice was in the company genes. As to the banana's genes, they were not doing too well, though their problems remained unknown to a world public that was increasing its demand for the fruit. But the Bunch, like the system of which it was part, had to keep growing and needed more outlets. Something stood in the way and the US government agreed to take the banana companies' case to the recently founded supreme court of globalisation, the World Trade Organisation (WTO).

Their problem was with Europe, not Eastern Europe, the former enemy, but Western Europe and capitalism's false friends in the Social Democracies. They had been allies of sorts since 1917, the year the US had entered the First World War and the Bolshevik revolution had occurred. Yet even now they persisted in their belief that they did not have to choose between Communism and capitalism and could stay living in their fool's paradise of a middle way. It was imperative that their stubbornness be broken down and that they be made to 'say uncle'.

What infuriated the Wild Bunch was that the West Europeans had set up a market that excluded rivals and they were also fixing prices, such crimes as were beyond redemption. The protected market was for former European colonies, some of them Caribbean islands. The West Europeans were paying the producers prices that were higher than those on the free market, in order, so they said, to help their ex-colonies develop. The fruit involved they called 'Fair Trade' bananas.

This was fundamentally wrong, from the Wild Bunch's view. Its members hailed from a distinguished tradition of free trade, nurtured and guarded throughout the years by United Fruit in its enclave. Hence, as the storm clouds gathered and both sides' bananas were put on a state of alert, the big companies from the Americas styled their fruit 'Free Trade' bananas.

The 'Free Traders' saw their case as unchallengeable because the prices they charged consumers, and those they paid their workers for their labour, were decided by the rigorous conditions of freedom. Certainly, their workers' wages seemed to have fallen drastically of late. Costa Rican plantation workers' pay in the 1990s had declined from about three dollars a day to two dollars fifty, the difference of fifty cents being a lot to a Costa Rican plantation worker. Then again, there were two important things to remember about this: firstly, that such workers were glad of the work – otherwise they would exercise their choice not to report to the plantation gate; secondly, that was how the free market was. The hidden hand made the decisions, not some interfering human agency. There was a phrase that summed it up: 'nothing personal, only business'.

There were other things wrong with the Fair Trade position, as viewed by liberated spirits pitched against them. 'Fair

Traders' professed benevolence yet, in claiming to be kind, were only being cruel. They were not letting their former subjects grow up. It was a jungle out there, it couldn't be denied, and it was getting to be more so. The former subject peoples would never be able to fend for themselves without throwing off the yolk of empire. The fact that they hadn't, furthermore, was only because of an historical anomaly. The Monroe Doctrine of 1823, had instructed foreigners to keep out of the Americas and let its peoples develop in the manner they chose. On sufferance a few imperial vestiges had remained in the region and now was the chance to drive them out. They should understand that they were no longer welcome: this was the enclave.

Strangely enough, the Grenada invasion a dozen or so years before in 1983 had made a similar point. As the US troops had dropped in on their pre-dawn tactical insertion and brought the island quickly under their control, Mrs Margaret Thatcher had complained to her friend President Ronald Reagan. This was Britain's sphere of influence, she had said. The president politely ignored her and carried on regardless. Grenada was a part of the world that Britain had only shared with United Fruit.

In the 1990s the real war broke out, the so-called 'Banana War' at the WTO. The US fought the case and what was at first a small skirmish over bananas escalated into general trade war. The US and Europe imposed bans and tariffs on hundreds of goods traded between them from bananas to coffee to bulls' semen. The Europeans blinked first at the dawn of a new millennium and in the face of what had been impressed upon them as the global realities. They retreated and agreed to phase out preferential treatment for their old colonies.

The companies that had assumed the historical mantle of United Fruit had won, having waged war as the old company had always claimed it did: in the name of the freedom of peoples. The Central American producer countries had little choice in their actions. They needed jobs for their people and had backed Chiquita and the rest.

The Europeans did not back down without rancour. The US government, they suggested, had allowed itself to be manipulated by narrow interests masquerading as beacons for a higher cause. It would not have been the first time, and someone among the Europeans referred to the 'old and dark forces'.

They might have detected that from behind the scenes the old company was shaking the curtain and laughing.

Epilogue: United Fruit World

United Fruit never left us. It went into a form of limbo, exiled to a place of suspension where souls might go to endure neither joy nor misery. It was put there to spare the system's further embarrassment and await its call to heaven. More than a company, United Fruit was an idea and at different times it was different things. Its functions ranged from being a force to combat the distant frontier to a machine that would bring the anarchy of capitalism under control. Lately United Fruit's spirit has revived as a means of taking capitalism into areas as yet unconquered.

Liberal capitalism in a purified form made its comeback as globalisation dawned upon us. Since the latter stages of the nineteenth century capitalism had suffered from hostile public opinion, laws to control its behaviour and taxes to help finance welfare states. In that time it was kept alive in isolated pockets like United Fruit's Central American enclave where its sturdy adherents stayed loyal to its dictates.

Now that we live in a boundless world, a strong body of opinion argues that the vehicle to drive globalisation across it is logically the multi-national corporation. Nation states are regarded as near useless in this process, confined as they are by their territorial boundaries. Only the multi-national has the global culture, runs this argument, only it 'speaks the language'.

United Fruit pioneered the multi-national spirit but it is debatable whether those that have followed it 'speak the language' any more than Minor Keith mastered Spanish. The burden of communication falls on others, as they have to do the talking and come up with the terms to keep the big companies there. As United Fruit showed when dealing with Guatemala over its railway a hundred years ago, the multinational company can always leave.

Today's world of the multi-national looks remarkably like the old one of United Fruit. Supporters of the big modern company say that in order to prosper it must be leaner and more streamlined. It must have its taxes cut and troublesome laws that hold it back removed. How else, they ask, can it compete with the new and thrusting forces, China and India? United Fruit would have relished such a low tax, low regulation world. That was what it always fought for.

Advocates of the new world cite John Locke, the English philosopher, who wondered in 1690 in his *Two Treatises of Government* what America must have first looked like to Columbus. Locke imagined a primitive paradise, a jungle free of interfering kings and dynasties with their laws and taxes and a whole new world to fashion. Locke's view was similar to that of Minor Keith as he looked down on the valleys of the Costa Rican interior in the late nineteenth century and saw his future stretched before him. Today's visionaries wonder whether we face a new moment of discovery in the manner of Locke, while they contrive to take Keith's view to its earthly extent. The process of globalisation amounts to United Fruit's enclave writ large.

They argue that it can go yet further. With the spirit of multi-national enterprise mankind can enter a new universe of possibilities. Harnessing the powers of molecular science, for example, would enable individuals to acquire extra inches in height, a new singing voice with which to soar, or whatever was wanted. Man could go beyond his genes. At the same time, it is worth recalling what happened after Keith looked out onto Costa Rica's verdant and pristine valleys. He carved out huge plantations of bananas and before long they were wracked with disease. One of their problems was their deep malaise in being unable to procreate. Whatever the enormous prospects currently being mapped out for mankind, the banana has never been able to go beyond its genes.

United Fruit scared so many people to death that it was eventually drummed from the scene. Until, as it were, the trouble had blown over, it was not talked about, for fear of provoking the wrong type of impressions of what big companies could get up to.

You can gauge this period of purdah by looking at the website of Chiquita, the surviving remnant of United Fruit that went off to Cincinnati for a new life and a new name. Chiquita is not the United Fruit of bygone times, though it bravely faces up to the past. It refers to it as 'Our Complex History', the use of 'complex' conveying a sense of pain and anguish and also some of the old company's art of the understated. Actually, several aspects of the chronology presented by Chiquita do not appear complex at all. Short references are made to events like the Santa Marta massacre of the late 1920s: 'Colombian army kills undetermined number of employees.' Balance is applied to the events of 1961, when United Fruit's Great White Fleet was represented at the Bay of Pigs invasion of Cuba, with a reference to 'United Fruit initiates sales of bananas to Japan'. Matters are even less complicated between 1975 and 1990 when nothing appears to have happened at all.

In the fifteen years from Eli Black's death to 1990, which Chiquita announces as the year in which it acquired its bright new name, everything went quiet. However, the good and open times when everyone could start talking in upbeat terms about multi-national corporations were just beginning. This was the year after the Berlin Wall came down and we all, in the East and West, joined our collective march to Banana Land.

United Fruit is not yet regarded as something to celebrate. It remains a lost Leviathan with evidence of it especially hard to find in its homeland. No New York memorial marks the spot where Black met his end and no statue commemorates Sam Zemurray trading on the New Orleans waterfront: 'Fifty stems, I'll take fifty!' United Fruit once put up a large hoarding on the Boston Long Wharf to commemorate the arrival of Andrew Preston and Captain Lorenzo Baker's first banana boat in 1871. Someone quietly removed the hoarding, possibly in the 1970s in the early stages of smartening up the Boston harbour area. Gentrification and the proletarian banana have not always been easy partners. The Massachusetts tourism authorities report some interest in reviving the old company's memory. They point out how, in the very early days when he retired from the hubbub of Boston to run matters from the Caribbean, Captain Baker opened hotels in Cape Cod and Jamaica and did much to get tourism under way in both.

You have to go elsewhere to trace the old company's legacy and in particular to Central America. Hundreds of thousands of people died in the wars of the 1980s and a million or so were left homeless. This caused a large increase in the number of illegal migrants to the US and contributed to the mounting social problems among the poorer communities of such cities as Los Angeles. The social disruption among those left at home includes generally sharp rises in crime and such a particular phenomenon as the violent, often murderous street gangs of San Salvador, membership of which includes children in their early teens.

Although this was not all United Fruit's fault, the company did little to encourage the forces of moderation and democracy. It persistently subverted them to create an atmosphere in which military regimes ruled and their death squads roamed the streets. In what had briefly promised to be a respite, in the late 1970s in Guatemala, I interviewed Manuel Colom Argueta, a Social Democrat who, it was said, had been favoured by President Jimmy Carter as the potential leader of a future civilian government in Guatemala. He spoke for a couple of hours, handed me copies of notes from his doctoral thesis on the troubled history of land ownership in Guatemala, in which United Fruit had obviously featured, and gave me a lift back from his office to the centre of town. Being a Social Democrat was a dangerous occupation in a United Fruit world, however, and Colom Argueta was murdered in his car in broad daylight by a death squad twelve days later.

Aside from the difficulties in building political stability from the rubble of such a past, economic and monetary dependency remain features of United Fruit's old domain. The banana enjoys a high rate of success in having those who come under its sway convert to using the dollar as their currency. Panama has long since used the US currency in its day-to-day transactions. Amid the economic insecurity that the banana uncannily seems to attract, Ecuador and El Salvador have recently abandoned their national currencies and Guatemala has considered doing so.

United Fruit had imagined its own memorial in Central America having such original features as building the railway in Costa Rica, draining the swamps of Limón and bringing street lighting to the capital, San José. By romantic expanses of nodding banana plants, it built company towns, brought jobs, general stores and the electricity for the Saturday night dance.

Yet so often it left devastation and the sense of a large uncaring force that had swept through. While hurricanes were an occupational hazard, United Fruit was a hurricane in its own way. It tramped on from dead plantation to soon-to-be dead plantation, leaving abandoned railroads, bridges and, according to one description, 'highlands of weeds'. Old company towns like Tela, in Honduras, remained, but retain a feeling of 'living in Macondo'. Former company offices in clapboard are often tattier than they were and could use another coat of malarial yellow.

Even the Costa Rican railroad that began the history of United Fruit has been closed. The line from the central plateau down to the Atlantic coast at Limón was expensive to maintain and its old blue locomotives stand rusting in abandoned sidings. Railways can prove remarkably difficult to run in the absence of state expenditure. Other expanses of Minor Keith's former railroad, in Guatemala, for example, have fallen into disrepair. Central America follows broadly the US public transport model whereby the better-off travel by air and the poorer by bus, if at all.

Poor communication in general is part of what the company left behind. Central America's Atlantic and Pacific coasts still tend not to talk to each other. English is relatively common among Atlantic communities in Costa Rica, Nicaragua and Guatemala, and Spanish predominates elsewhere.

If United Fruit helped 'export' slave-like conditions of work from the US, where they were no longer tolerated, it subsequently played its part in creating practices and routines which would become acceptable for importing back into the US. On the Central American plantations and at the dockside sirens summoned workers as ships arrived at any hour of the day and night. When the work was done, labourers were stood down until summoned again. Such methods are being tried today in some industries in developed countries – fast-food outlets, for example – and are usually described as among the requirements for a modern flexible workforce.

Following its disappearance, the story of United Fruit was put away for safe keeping and forgotten. Part of its memorial today can still be found locked up in the vaults of the Harvard Business School in Cambridge, Massachusetts, where an excellent collection of photographs is kept by the school's Baker Library. From the comprehensive photographic record of United Fruit's works through many years of its life, you can sense how the old company enjoyed its power in Central America. Men in high boots stride the plantations from Belize to Colombia. Waistcoated overseers supervise the gangs loading stems of bananas into railroad cars. Even the Banana Six jazz band has been saved for posterity, with their slicked-back hair, cufflinked long sleeves and collection of instruments, in a photograph taken shortly before the company abandoned the Honduran port of Puerto Castilla to disease in the 1930s. In one photo taken a quarter of a century later, a collection of alternative products to the banana are lined up on display for visiting chiefs from Boston. Among the various fruits and plants is a spray of coca leaves. In the 1960s United Fruit battled frantically against the idea of the banana having any hallucinogenic qualities, yet at one stage had thought of going into the cocaine business. It rethought and stuck with monoculture.

In the meticulous way it has been compiled, United Fruit's photographic collection shows that the company itself wanted to be remembered. It would be churlish now not to comply with its wishes.

United Fruit fought wars from the Honduran invasion of 1911 to Guatemala in 1954, or it had others do battle on its behalf, as in Colombia in 1928. In the 1930s, General Smedley Butler cited the 'rape' of the Central American republics, in which he and the marines were involved. The company's narrow pursuit of its business interests had huge international repercussions. The attempt to repeat the Guatemalan exercise of 1954 at the Bay of Pigs in 1961 led to the Cuban missile crisis of 1962. The thinking behind the idea that Fidel Castro would topple as a result of the Bay of Pigs received a repeat run in the case of Iraq forty years later. The anticipated cheers and celebrations for the Iraq invasion were also echoes from the US's successful intervention in United Fruit's old Caribbean territory of Grenada in 1983.

As United Fruit went about expanding its empire, however, it did not always have to bludgeon its way in. It showed how countries might slip into dependency on large companies. It worked its way into the fabric of Costa Rican and Guatemalan society by invitation because it had the resources that these countries lacked.

Like multi-national companies today, United Fruit made alliances when and where it could to survive. It sought out malleable elements: politicians with whom it could cut a deal and presidents-in-exile awaiting their call to sail back to power. United Fruit might even help find a boat. Its efforts showed that as long as it did not unduly offend the contemporary mores of its home base, then it could probably get away with much overseas. Its levels of bribery in Honduras in the 1920s did prompt a debate in the US Congress, which concluded that that was the way business was done in such parts of the world.

United Fruit's practices remain much valued in today's business world. 'Propaganda' tends not to be a term used quite so bluntly as it was by United Fruit's spin guru, Edward Bernays, but his own alternative, 'public relations', suffices nicely. Advertising, the creation of demand and primacy of form over content were company specialities. The banana has for a century been a first-rate example of 'packaging': it exudes health in its natural wrapping while being diseased to its roots. United Fruit took the primitive art of 'branding' to a higher stage when it stuck its Señorita Chiquita label on its bananas in the 1950s.

United Fruit championed the theory of 'hearts and minds' before the term came into use. It set out to 'get 'em young' as it made its way into schools. Its efforts in film-making in 1954 were effective propaganda back-up to the coup in Guatemala. As late as 1969, it was still sending educational kits on its work into classrooms and, at $4 a time, making money from them. It was well ahead of its time in trying to encourage American mothers to break their strict three-meals-a-day routine by having them feed bananas to their children 'between times'. The company had disappeared from view before the 'graze all day' habit became the norm but it had helped pave the way for others to take full advantage.

A formidable force in the art of political lobbying, United Fruit employed some of the most skilled 'purveyors of concentrated influence'. Then it went further, by making sure it was on the 'inside' and connected to the top people in government. Others have continued the practice into modern times. The late Kenneth Lay, head of Enron, the large energy company, was 'Kenny' to President George W. Bush, though he was dumped in 2001 when he and Enron fell into disgrace.

The key legacy of United Fruit is that we worry about multi-national corporations. What is the role of large US defence contractors in Iraq or the oil companies in Nigeria? We assume that corporations would not engineer coups and invasions as United Fruit did. Then we learn of the aborted coup in Equatorial Guinea in 2003, where individual adventurers attempted to seize power in the small, oil-rich West African country imagining that governments and other interests would back them when presented with a fait accompli. This was much the same with Sam Zemurray's exploits alongside those of Lee Christmas and 'Machine-gun' Molony in Honduras in 1911.

As a prime example of a 'nasty trust', United Fruit is the reason behind laws regulating the behaviour of large companies. This argument riles business people who say it is unduly sceptical. Life has changed, they say, corporate standards have improved and today's multi-national bosses are decent people. But then in an imaginative world, suddenly something happens that shocks us. This often comes when there has been a downturn in economic fortunes which, in turn, causes us to reassess the virtue of the times. One company or another and its highly regarded boss is charged with an outrage that no one has quite foreseen and, as a result, everyone feels deceived. It happened with Eli Black as it happened with Enron's Kenneth Lay.

★ ★ ★

Black had jumped in the nick of time. When he died other big companies had been acting in the abusive way of the old robber barons and of the old United Fruit. There was a great deal of concern in the mid-1970s about what the world would be like if big companies continued to act in this manner and there was much discussion of what action should be taken to curb them. Policy makers wondered whether it was time to reassert control on behalf of nation states, some even suggesting the need to 'seize the commanding heights' of their economies.

The road to redemption for the big companies would take some while to complete yet their journey began almost immediately. The international oil companies were at the forefront. By midway through 1975 the oil price rises from the Middle East war two years before had caused general inflation of crisis proportions. Inflation at that time in the UK, for example, reached 25 per cent, a level more appropriate, as was pointed out at the time, to a banana republic.

Economic theorists concluded that it was time for a dramatic change in policy. In particular, costs would have to be cut in state spending on schools, hospitals and other areas of the welfare state. Such thinking was in line with the theory of monetarism, devised by Professor Milton Friedman in the rarified academic enclave of the University of Chicago. Monetarism was extremely unpopular at first and to put it into practice required conditions of tight security that United Fruit would have envied on its Central American plantations. They were provided by General Augusto Pinochet in Chile who came to power in his United Fruit-style coup and, as United Fruit had in Central America, turned his country into a laboratory for an exercise in capitalist economics.

Monetarism gained a democratic respectability of sorts when it was adopted by Margaret Thatcher after her election in Britain in 1979, though it still needed a war to boost its chances of survival. Mrs Thatcher would probably have lost the next UK election had it not been for her comprehensive victory against Argentina in the Falklands war of 1982. As a result of it, she also became closely allied with Argentina's neighbour and enemy, Chile's General Pinochet. In 1981 President Reagan had come to the White House and straightaway had formed a close working relationship with Mrs Thatcher. By the end of the decade the Cold War was won with free market thinking ascendant.

There were still some tricky moments for it to endure. With the economy in another of its slumps, George Bush Senior, Reagan's successor, tried to boost his domestic support by a familiar tactic: he invaded old United Fruit territory in Central America. His successful efforts in 1988 to remove the renegade regime of General Manuel Noriega in Panama, however, did not win him the next election. Bill Clinton came to the White House arguing that the problem was 'the economy, stupid' and that capitalism should be put under review. Something was required to address the system's anarchic way of moving between booms and slumps, he suggested, some form of planning, perhaps. Clinton later abandoned the effort, perceiving the need to get the economy moving quickly again when planning just promised to be laborious. The US and the world, therefore, went for the full capitalist anarchy option, namely globalisation.

At the new millennium the banana industry's Wild Bunch marked the moment of triumph with their victory over the Fair Trade Europeans at the WTO. With supporters of the new way enraptured, the multi-national corporation was perceived as the star that would guide the world to globalisation. Thus, the multi-national, as an institution, completed a remarkable transformation, such that you might never have known it had ever been a problem. In twenty-five years, it had gone from capitalism's pariah to apparent saviour of the system.

With the multi-national in steering position, its supporters imagine nation states will give way to new forms. The old welfare state will disappear alongside its protections, guarantees and interferences in the free market mechanism. One potential successor that is gaining strong support is that of the 'market state', a supremely competitive entity within which the multi-national will be unleashed to achieve its full powers and, it is claimed, mankind's potential.

By current standards, this is not an extreme way of thinking. One of its leading US proponents, Philip Bobbitt, has been an adviser to Democratic and Republican administrations alike. In his book *The Shield of Achilles* he addresses the all enveloping question of how the world is to be governed. The broad answer appears to be by the US and its large companies. As the nearest thing in the world to a 'market state', the US is ahead of the pack and must turn its strategic thinking to making the decisions that will boost its multinationals.

Central Americans already have an instinctive grasp of what this could mean. In United Fruit's old part of the globe, the free market has been given its head over a more sustained period than anywhere else. The market state would not guarantee the wellbeing of its people because that would be up to them. The new order would be the undeniably exciting one that would 'maximise the opportunities of societies and individuals'. The stodgy welfare society, in all its mediocrity, would be replaced by an 'opportunity society'.

It is in this context that the multi-nationals would be scheduled to get their tax cuts and have the regulations that bind their freedom of action removed. As to their future behaviour, that would not be guarded by laws but by mature self-regulation. In fact, lest we worry, the mechanism is already in place. Established practice among multi-nationals of the new enlightenment, this comes in the form of the doctrine of 'Corporate Social Responsibility'.

This is the buzz phrase of the age and everyone who is corporately anyone is doing it. Bill Gates pours his Microsoft billions into charitable work. Starbucks is helping coffee farmers in Kenya. One of the most interesting cases is Chiquita, which has won praise in the *Financial Times* and other esteemed media for its work with the Rainforest Alliance, the conservation group based in New York dedicated to protecting the environment through good business practice. On the face of it, one conclusion that could be drawn is that if a company with United Fruit in its background can practise responsible business, then any company can and probably does.

This is not necessarily so. Only a small and visible minority of companies have 'signed up' to the contemporary code of best behaviour. The majority carry on as before in a United Fruit way, particularly in developing countries. Only when scandals unfold do we become aware. A diligent labour organisation from the US might have gone down to scrabble through rubbish tips in Honduras to unearth the pay slips that reveal the slave- wage realities. A distressed celebrity who lent his or her name to the T-shirt or trainers appears in a press conference to express mortification at learning that the disgraced item has been manufactured under sweatshop conditions.

The truth is that even the good Corporate Social Responsibility companies are acting like United Fruit. While their intentions may be honourable they follow in a long tradition laid down by none other than United Fruit itself. From the Mayan ruins of Quiriguá to the rubble of Managua, the company acted as a philanthropist. It gave endowments for the advancement of women at university, the protection of children and facilities for the higher education of Central American agriculturalists. After providing relief to victims of the 1972 Nicaraguan earthquake, it was Eli Black who referred to 'Our Social Responsibility'. He almost coined the very term that is so popular today.

United Fruit also made a point of engaging the services of the best people. These included some of Boston's finest families, ambassadors to the United Nations, heads of the intelligence services, high-ranking churchmen and secretaries of state. John Foster Dulles, to name but one, was one of the most esteemed international statesmen of his age and would not have allied himself with an entity so readily dismissed as a nasty trust. In its time United Fruit embodied Corporate Social Responsibility and by its actions might reasonably have claimed to have invented it. None of that was a guarantee against its abuses.

We continually put ourselves in a position to be surprised. We assume the best, elevate people to pedestals and celebrate their friendship with presidents. We are shocked when it is revealed that we have been 'sold' a lie. Then we get embarrassed and try to forget, as we did with United Fruit.

Those that argue the case for the unleashed multi-national may not intend to but would have us 'say uncle' to huge global forces over whom we'd have no control, except through our minimal influence as individuals in the market place. We would have to trust those forces to behave in line with vague notions of Corporate Social Responsibility, of which United Fruit always claimed to be a principled practitioner. Today's advocates of multi-national power would have us all as banana republics.

Costa Rica is the case of one that knows. Other Central American neighbours who had fallen into banana republicanism and tried to escape it have been violently prevented from doing so. Guatemala and Nicaragua are two such examples. Costa Rica successfully fled banana republicanism by establishing its welfare state only to find it is being pulled back by the forces of globalisation.

Since the 1950s Costa Rica has transformed itself into a haven from the rigours of life elsewhere in Central America. It has reduced the number of people living in poverty from a half to a fifth of its population of four million. It has introduced better schools, health care and laws to aid the security of workers. The number of people able to read and write rose to 96 per cent, a rate that compares favourably with that of richer countries. Life expectancy is seventy-eight years, one higher than in the US.

Pressures to compete in the global market have brought change over recent years. The state has had to reduce its expenditure on facilities like public hospitals. Costa Rica's emphasis on social equality is breaking down, with incomes of the richest people doubling since the late 1980s and those of the poorest rising by less than a tenth. Begging is common in Central

America but has not been so in Costa Rica. Lately, the number of beggars on the streets has been noticeably increasing, as has that of prostitutes. Gambling is on the rise. Costa Rica is perhaps best known for its eco-paradise of forests, national parks and wildlife refuges. Such protected areas amount to about a quarter of national territory. Environmentalists are concerned about the extent to which these may yet be subjected to 'rational' economic development.

Costa Ricans worry especially about one pivotal aspect of civic life they had come to take for granted, the incorruptibility of their politicians. There have been a number of cases of alleged corruption of late involving leading figures. One left the country rapidly for Switzerland and others have faced charges of embezzlement and accepting bribes from a multi-national.

This is not the Costa Rica of recent generations and the prospects for the country that took on the leviathan of United Fruit and won look daunting. As one local commentator put it, 'we are returning to Central America.'

The fate of the product that United Fruit gave the world is the final testament to the company's work and ways. As a clone, the banana suffers its extreme genetic weakness. Mass production and monoculture have proved too much of an added burden. The huge plantations of the past century have enabled disease to take hold over wide areas and sweep on. With only one variety to chew through, the banana's pathogenic enemies have been able to get on with their work without having to adapt to new and different challenges.

The banana companies gave up experimenting to find new types of banana some twenty years ago. They concentrated on fighting the banana's adversaries with intensified chemical warfare. It was too difficult and expensive to find enough decent seeds in bananas to engender new ones, they argued, because they had to compete in the world and keep their prices down. The ailing banana had itself become a welfare issue too far.

Private enterprise pushed the fruit's fate back onto the resources of impoverished states. The scientists skilled in genetic modification were summoned and only too pleased to be invited. More recently the companies have resumed the quest for seeds and new breeds in the collective hope that a truly disease-resistant variety can be found this time. No word has emerged of a banana breakthrough.

The issue with the fruit is not whether it should be sold 'Free Trade' or 'Fair Trade' but how much longer it will be sold at all. In our case, the world's progress indicates that those in charge of the unseen mechanism have mapped out our path. Strangely, it is similar to that of the banana. As it heads back to its origins in the forest, so we are bound for Banana Land and our United Fruit world of jungle capitalism.

Select Bibliography

Adams, Frederick Upham. *Conquest of the Tropics: The Story of the Creative Enterprises Conducted by the United Fruit Company.* Doubleday, Page & Company, New York, 1914

Amory, Cleveland. *The Proper Bostonians.* E.P. Dutton & Co., New York, 1947

Anderson, Jon Lee. *Che Guevara: A Revolutionary Life.* Bantam Press, 1997

Asturias Miguel Ángel. *The Green Pope.* Delacorte, New York, 1971. Originally published 1954

Bakan, Joel. *The Corporation: The Pathological Pursuit of Profit and Power.* Constable & Robinson, 2004

Baker, Ernest H. 'United Fruit'. *Fortune*, March 1933

Bernays, Edward L. *Biography of an Idea.* Simon and Schuster, New York, 1965

Bernays, Edward L. *Propaganda.* Liveright, New York, 1928

Bobbit, Philip. *The Shield of Achilles; War, Peace and the Course of History.* Penguin, 2003

Bourgois, Philippe. *Ethicity at Work:Divided Labour on a Central American Banana Plantation.* Johns Hopkins University, Baltimore, 1989

Bucheli, Marcelo. *United Fruit Company and Local Politics in Colombia 1900–1970.* Draft for Comments: Department of History, Stanford University, 1997

Butler, Smedley D. *War is a Racket.* Feral House, Los Angeles, 2003. Originally published in 1935

Cabot, Thomas. *Beggar on Horseback.* David R. Godine, Boston, 1979

Crowther, Samuel. *The Romance and Rise of the Tropics.* Doubleday and Duran, New York, 1929

Cullather, Nick. *Secret History: The CIA's Classified Account of Its Operations in Guatemala, 1952–54.* With afterword by Piero Gleijeses. Stanford University, 1999

Deutsch, Hermann B. *The Incredible Yanqui: The Career of Lee Christmas.* Longmans, Green and Co, London, New York, 1931

Dosal, Paul J. *Doing Business with the Dictators: A Political History of United Fruit in Guatemala, 1899–1944.* Scholarly Resources, Wilmington, Delaware, 1993

García Márquez, Gabriel. *One Hundred Years of Solitude.* Penguin, 1972. Originally published in 1967

Halberstam, David. *The Fifties*. Fawcett, New York, 1994

Henry, O. *Cabbages and Kings*. Penguin, 1993. Originally published in 1904

Hunt, E. Howard. *Undercover: Memoirs of an American Secret Agent*. Berkley Publishing, 1974

Immerman, Richard H. *The CIA in Guatemala: The Foreign Policy of Intervention*. University of Texas Press, 1982

Jenkins, Virginia Scott. *Bananas: An American History*. Smithsonian Institution Press, 2000

Karnes, Stanley. *Tropical Enterprise: The Standard Fruit and Steamship Company in Latin America*. Louisiana State University, 1938

Kepner, Charles, and Soothill, Jay. *The Banana Empire: A Case Study of Banana Imperialism*. Russell & Russell, New York, 1963. Originally published in 1935

Kinzer, Stephen. 'The Trouble with Costa Rica'. *The New York Review*, June 8, 2006

Kobler, John. 'Sam the Banana Man'. *Life*, February, 1951

Litvin, Daniel. *Empires of Profit: Commerce, Conquest and Corporate Responsibility*. TEXERE, London, New York, 2003

McCann, Thomas. *An American Company: The Tragedy of United Fruit*. Crown Publishers, 1976

McCullough, David. *The Path Between the Seas: The Creation of the Panama Canal*. Simon and Schuster, 1977

McQueen, Humphrey. *The Essence of Capitalism*. Profile, 2001

Melville, John H. *The Great White Fleet*. Vantage, New York, 1979

Munro, Dana. *Intervention and Dollar Diplomacy in the Caribbean, 1900–1921*. Princeton University, 1964

Niedergang, Marcel. *The Twenty Latin Americas* (Volume 1). Penguin, 1971

Pearce, Fred. 'Going Bananas'. *New Scientist*, January 18, 2003

Pringle, Henry. 'A Jonah Who Swallowed the Whale'. *American Magazine*, September 1933

Schlesinger, Stephen, and Kinzer, Stephen. *Bitter Fruit: The Story of the American Coup in Guatemala*. Harvard University, 1999

Solow, Herbert. 'The Ripe Problems of United Fruit'. *Fortune*, March 1959

Soluri, John. *Banana Cultures: Agriculture, Consumption & Environmental Change in Honduras and the United States*. University of Texas Press, 2005

United Fruit Historical Society. *www.unitedfruit.org*

Warner, Marina. *No Go the Bogeyman: Scaring, Lulling and Making Mock*. Farrar, Strauss and Giroux, 1998

Whitfield, Stephen. 'Strange Fruit: The Career of Samuel Zemurray'. *American Jewish History*, March 1984

Wilson, Charles Morrow. *Empire in Green and Gold: The Story of the American Banana Trade*. Greenwood, New York, 1968. Originally published in 1947

Index

INDEX

INDEX

INDEX

INDEX